OPERATING
RADIO CONTROL
ENGINES

Other titles in this series include:

Installing Radio Control Equipment   Peter Smoothy
Building From Plans   David Boddington
Setting Up Radio Control Helicopters   Dave Day
Basic Radio Control Flying   David Boddington
Flying Scale Gliders   Chas Gardiner
Moulding and Glass fibre Techniques   Peter Holland
Covering Model Aircraft   Ian Peacock

Operating
Radio Control
Engines

Brian Winch and
David Boddington

ARGUS BOOKS

Argus Books
Wolsey House
Wolsey Road
Hemel Hempstead
Hertfordshire HP2 4SS

First published by Argus Books 1989

© Brian Winch and David Boddington 1989

ISBN 0 85242 986 X

Phototypesetting by GCS, Leighton Buzzard
Printed and bound in Great Britain by
William Clowes Ltd, Beccles

Contents

	Foreword	6
CHAPTER 1	Introduction—engine types	7
CHAPTER 2	How an engine works	15
CHAPTER 3	After-purchase preparation and running in	23
CHAPTER 4	Installing and operating the engine in a model	31
CHAPTER 5	Fault finding	39
CHAPTER 6	Care and maintenance	43
CHAPTER 7	Propeller selection	49
CHAPTER 8	Fuels	55
APPENDIX 1	Examples of typical engines	61
Index		63

Foreword

YOU WILL notice that this handbook has a combined authorship of Brian Winch, from the Southern hemisphere, and David Boddington, from the Northern hemisphere. Now, this is not because engines run differently in England from those in Australia; it is quite wrong to assume that the propellers of I.C. model engines turn in a clockwise direction on the southern side of the equator! If, like the bathwater, the rotation direction changed between the hemispheres what would happen as the model flew over the equator?

No, the reason for the dual authorship is simply a matter of expediency where Brian feeds in the 'nitty gritty' of the practical aspects and David adds some of the general comments and sews the package together.

The handbook has been published to give advice to novices—and more experienced R/C modellers—to allow them to get the best service, reliability and performance from their engines. When you purchase a model engine, new or second-hand, you are making an investment. Properly respected and maintained that investment will keep its value and you will have an engine that will give you continuing good performance and will not let you down at crucial moments.

Go to any powered model flying event and you will be able to detect the participants who are knowledgeable about engines and have taken care of them. They will *not* be the ones that are fiddling about with the carburettors to get the last bit of performance from the engine; the competent engine operators will be the ones who start their engines with a minimum of fuss, carry out a few vital checks and go out to fly a full tankful of fuel with never a worry about the engine quitting. Our object is to provide the information to allow YOU to reach this level of competence.

Chapter 1
Introduction—
Engine types

PERHAPS WE should clarify a couple of terms straight away. What is the difference between, in model terms, an engine and a motor? As far as I am aware, there is no difference. Certainly you will not hear mention of an electric engine or, for that matter, a jet motor, but these are related to convention rather than definitions. We may lapse from the term engine to that of motor throughout the text—it has no particular significance.

Two of the most expensive items you will buy for your hobby are engines and radio equipment. What you purchase in these departments will have a direct influence on the types and sizes of the models you build and fly. We therefore have the situation where we can select the model to suit the equipment we already have or, conversely, buy the engine and radio to meet the requirements of the chosen model. If finances were no object, then the latter solution would be ideal. Most of us have strict monetary limitations when it comes to spending on luxury (essential?) items and we must therefore work in reverse— select a model design to match our existing equipment, particularly the engine. Experienced modellers may be contemplating the acquisition of addi-

Typical of the modern generation of two-stroke glow engines, the OS FP series are economically priced, but are of high quality and give high performance.

tional equipment—reading these words may help you to save money and obtain more fun per pound spent.

Selecting the engine

Electric-powered models are dealt with in separate publications so we will restrict ourselves to I.C. (Internal Combustion) engines. There is a bewildering variety of engines on the market and it is difficult enough for the established modeller to keep track of the types of designations: for the newcomer it is, without some guidance, nearly impossible. So, how do you make your selection of a suitable engine? By a process of elimination. Before going to your local model shop, or writing off to a mail order company, set down your requirements. If your thoughts are so vague as to make it difficult to list these needs, perhaps the following general descriptions will assist you in coming to the correct conclusions.

There are three principal forms of ignition used in model engines.

Glow (or Glo) engines

The glow engine incorporates a plug with a coil of platinum wire (element) built into the barrel of the plug body. To start the glow engine the element must be heated by an external battery source, until it is glowing brightly. When the crankshaft is rotated, by flicking the propeller or applying an electric starter, the heated plug will ignite the fuel/air mixture and the engine will start. Once running, and the fuel setting correctly adjusted with the needle valve, the external power source can be disconnected. Ignition, with the battery removed, is continued by the process of the compression of the firing stroke being sufficient to maintain the glow of the plug, thus allowing ignition of the fuel mixture on subsequent revolutions.

There is no doubt that the basic simplicity of the two-stroke glow engine, its light weight and high power output potential have led to it becoming the most popular form of model engine. It has been commercially produced in sizes from .010 cu.in. capacity to engines one hundred times this size. Carburettors offering good throttle control and response are available on all but the smallest capacities, i.e. from .049 cu. in. (.8cc) upwards. Non-R/C (without a carburettor) glow engines have only one adjustable control, the fuel needle-valve.

Fuel for glow motors is a mixture of methanol and oil (castor or synthetic) and nitromethane can also be added to improve the power output; it also improves the smoothness of running with smaller capacity engines.

Four-stroke glow engines

A relatively new phenomenon, although an old principle, four-stroke glow engines were introduced commercially over ten years ago and their popularity was, to a large extent, unforeseen.

One of the earliest and most popular of all diesel engines was the Mills 1.3cc. Replicas of this and the .75cc version are still being made.

Coinciding with a greater awareness of noise pollution, the four-stroke offered quieter operation, better fuel consumption and, for the scale enthusiast and vintage modeller, a more authentic sound. Due to the greater complexities of the construction of the four-stroke engine, the price was also considerably higher.

With the quest for increased power outputs the modern generation of four-strokes are noisier than their predecessors and a silencer is now mandatory. So what advantages does the four-stroke motor offer? They are undeniably a pleasant sounding engine, even at equivalent decibel levels to the two-stroke; they offer better fuel consumption and can swing a large diameter propeller at relatively slow r.p.m. In fairness it should be possible to achieve most of these aims with a two-stroke engine—at considerably lower cost. The older cross-flow ported engines, particularly long-stroke types, will give nearly as good a fuel consumption and the silencing can be improved by fitting a more effective silencer (home-made or an add-on unit) and these engines also operate at lower rpm than the Schneurle ported engines. Costs are much lower and, being simpler, they are easier to operate and maintain. Nor do they suffer from the bearing corrosion associated with four-stroke engines. However, they are not readily available and the four-stroke will continue to be desirable from a noise consideration.

Diesels

At one time in Britain, in the 1950s, model diesel engines outnumbered glow motors by a considerable margin. This state of affairs gradually reversed until, now, diesel engines account for only a small percentage of the engines used in R/C model aeroplanes (and I have yet to see one used in an R/C helicopter).

Leading to the decline in the use of diesels were two factors; the demand for larger capacity engines (where the diesels were less tractable and smooth-running) and the inability to obtain reliable throttle response under all conditions—usually a failure to increase speed after prolonged idling. The former objection still applies and few diesels are available in capacities over 5cc, although diesel conversions are available for larger-sized motors. With modern engine technology the problems of obtaining good throttle response have been overcome and even the small (1cc) diesel motors have acceptable throttle control.

One further reason why diesels may not be so readily accepted is the fact that they have two variable controls, the needle valve and the compression screw. No ignition plug is used with a diesel: it relies on the compression between the piston and contra-piston to ignite the atomised fuel/air mixture. To achieve this a fuel containing ether is used, mixed with paraffin and lubricating oil. It has to be admitted that the exhaust fumes from this fuel mixture are fairly pungent and pervasive—although, to

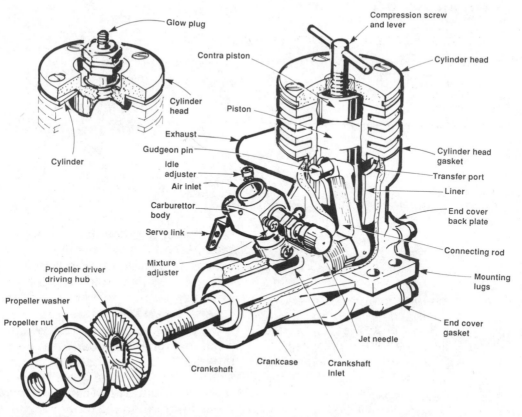

Typical I.C. model two-stroke engine showing the alternative diesel and glow combustion.

the long-established modeller, it is a smell that is full of nostalgia and more akin to perfume!

Starting a diesel engine does require a specific technique. It is often necessary to increase the compression screw for starting and the propeller must be given a smart flick to take it over the compression stroke fast enough to make it fire. Electric starters are not recommended with small capacity diesels. When flooded (too large a fuel content in the crankcase) there is the risk of damaging the engine with prolonged application of a starter. You have to develop a 'feel' for diesel starting, knowing when it is over-compressed or under-compressed, flooded or dry, and this is only obtained from a little experience. Unfortunately, the hardest

engine to start is often a new one straight out of its box. Modellers have been known to 'write off' diesel engines without ever achieving a start and giving them a fair trial.

Diesel engines should not be ignored as suitable power plants for small and medium sized models. They are quiet, very economic on fuel consumption, will swing unbelievably large propellers at very low rpm and their non-R/C versions offer much greater flexibility than glow engines. In return, you must be prepared to spend a little more time understanding the operation of the diesel engine. If you have starting problems with a new engine ask an experienced (old?) aeromodeller for assistance; he will take great pleasure in showing you how to get it running.

Spark ignition

More commonly known as 'petrol engines', the spark ignition motor virtually disappeared with the advent of the glowplug and diesel engines. It has now re-emerged, but only in larger capacity engines. Bonuses with spark ignition motors are the cheap fuel (petrol/oil mix) excellent fuel consumption figures, very clean burning and good power outputs at modest rpm. Against this are the disadvantages of greater complexities, with magnetos, coils, (or electronic ignition) and batteries, all adding to the overall weight. Costs are also greater initially, although these may be offset with the lower running costs for modellers doing a lot of flying.

Electronic Spark ignition systems available now, for conversion of glow engines, may be incorporated in purpose-designed engines, making the 'petrol engine' a popular choice once again. As with glow motors, spark ignition can apply equally to two or four-stroke engines.

Engine layouts

In addition to the various types of ignition used in model engines there is also a variety of engine layouts. The most common is undoubtedly a single cylinder, front induction, side exhaust, direct crankshaft drive layout. Single cylinder engines may also have rear induction and/or rear exhaust configurations and it is also possible to purchase integrally geared units. Multi-cylinder motors (two to seven cylinders) are also available, not unnaturally at considerably higher retail prices. For the sports, or fun, flyer these exotic and expensive motors can hardly be justified.

Fox Tartan engine can be supplied in spark ignition or glow forms. Note the pump type carburettor fitted on one side and non-model style silencer on opposite side.

Glossary of terms

Size—referred to in measurements of cubic inches, or cubic centimetres, of the swept volume. Thus an '049' engine has a capacity of .049 cu.in. or .8 cc approx. Smaller diesel engines are usually designated in ccs and a '15' diesel can refer to 1.5 cc capacity; glow engines are normally sized in cu.ins. Therefore, a '15' in this instance refers to a .15 cu.in. (2.5cc) capacity.

S or Schneurle Porting—a method of cylinder porting (transfer of fuel mixture from the crankcase to the combustion chamber) introduced to improve performance. A similar system is known as PDP (Perry Directional Porting) and, in common with Schneurle porting, is designed to realise the maximum output of the engines. Engines that do not have these designations can generally be assumed to have cross-flow scavenged porting more modest in design performance but, together with suitable bore/stroke ratios, may produce a lower 'revving' motor with high torque values. Consequently, the Schneurle ported engines are normally of the high performance and racing types (turning small propellers at very high speeds) used in competititve models. Cross-flow type engines are lower in price, involving

11

less expensive machining costs, lower in maximum outputs but probably capable of swinging larger diameter propellers at slower speeds (more applicable to sports and scale models).

Lapped Piston—where the external surfaces of the piston are in direct contact with the cylinder wall the precise fit of the piston/cylinder assembly is achieved by 'lapping'. Engines with lapped pistons may require more running in than with other types (the exceptions being the very small glow engines where the machined fits are to extremely close tolerances) and they are generally restricted to engines under the capacity of '35s' (5.75 cc). After careful running-in they should give excellent service and long life—you will need to do a lot of flying to wear out the average 'sports' engine. It is only when high performance engines are run under maximum speed conditions that problems are likely to arise.

Ringed pistons—for many years it was standard practice to fit larger capacity model engines with twin cast iron piston rings but these have now been largely superseded by a single Dykes style piston ring. Because of the considerably reduced mass of metal in contact with the cylinder wall the amount of running-in time is greatly reduced compared with a lapped piston. Although ringed pistons have lost favour to the ABC and AAC piston/cylinder assemblies there is nothing wrong with this form of piston seal and they are more than adequate for all but the very high performance contest motors.

ABC—stands for Aluminium piston and Chromed Brass cylinder liner. The coefficients of expansion of these materials are such that, as the engine warms up, good compression is retained and the friction between the piston and cylinder wall remains low. You can usually tell whether an engine has an

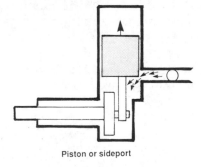

Piston or sideport

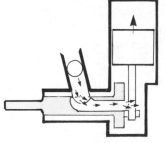

Front rotary

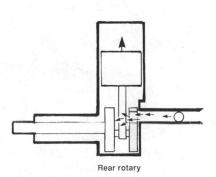

Rear rotary

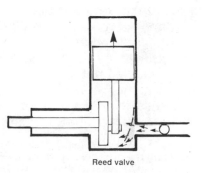

Reed valve

Types of induction used on model engines.

ABC piston/liner (or AAC) by turning the engine over by hand; there is a definite tightening of the piston as it goes over top dead centre, even to the extent of it being 'squeaky' tight.

AAC—Similar to ABC, and have the same benefits, but have an aluminium liner with chrome deposit surface. Little running-in is required with the AAC and ABC engines, they can be taken out of the box and fitted straight into a model (providing care is taken to keep the engines slightly rich for the first few flights). Production costs cause them to be associated with the higher performance, higher cost engines.

Stunt—engines not fitted with RC carburettors, i.e. for free flight or control-line applications, may also be referred to as 'standard' engines.

Car—manufactured for use in R/C cars and land vehicles.

H or Heli—designed for installation in R/C helicopters.

P—for pylon racing models, not normally supplied with an R/C carburettor.

Model engines can be supplied in a variety of induction styles and the exhaust outlets may also be positioned to the side (normal) to rear or, very occasionally (usually for boats) with front exhaust. Engine at top is front induction, rear exhaust, standard (i.e. non R/C) engine. Centre is rear induction and exhaust, and lower and left is the more normal front induction, side exhaust layouts—both without R/C carburettors.

DF—produced for specialised ducted fan models, i.e. for high speed operation using a multi-bladed fan instead of the more conventional propellers.

Marine—fitted with a water cooled cylinder head for use in boats, or water cooled engines in aeroplanes!

RC—fitted with a carburettor for throttle control.

F or FI—front induction, with the carburettor fitted at the front of the engine.

R or RI—rear induction, with the carburettor fitted at the rear of the engine.

SE—side exhaust, the exhaust stack positioned at the side of the engine. Usually on the right hand side (viewed from the rear with the engine upright).

RE—rear exhaust—normally restricted to marine engines; it is a less convenient layout for model aeroplanes.

Plain—plain crankshaft bearings, more usually associated with the smaller and less expensive engines. Plain bearing engines, in sizes up to '35' capacity, are capable of giving many hundreds of hours of trouble-free service in normal usage.

BB—ball race versions, normally fitted to the front and rear of the crankshaft to improve efficiency and smooth running.

LS—Long stroke; some manufacturers are now reverting to longer stroke/bore ratio versions of their engines for the benefit of scale modellers (turning larger diameter propellers at low revolutions) and in the interests of reducing noise levels (quite high proportions of the total noise level are attributable to the propeller and lower speeds means lower noise levels for aerobatic models).

G—geared, another method of enabling the engine to turn larger propellers at reduced speeds, recommended for large, heavily loaded R/C models.

X—Not a specific definition but usually denotes a higher performance engine where the manufacturer has a similar capacity standard engine in the range.

Enya use the designation S.S. (Super Sport) for their range of lapped pistons, plain bearing and ball-raced engines. O.S. use the term FSR for Schneurle ported and FP for their plain bearing lapped piston motors.

Modern engines are, for the most part, superbly engineered and beautifully packaged. It is all to easy to be seduced by the object itself and to forget the purpose of the engine. However desirable an engine may be the reason for buying it is to power a radio control model and the purchase should be made with this sole intention. Do not be talked into buying an engine that is unsuitable for your needs, it is not always a question of the most expensive automatically being the best.

Chapter 2
How an engine works

TERMINOLOGY FOR engine parts is generally universal. However, there has been some controversy about the terminology of the four-stroke engine, i.e. should it be more correctly described as a four-cycle engine? Sufficient to say that the term 'four-cycle', although commonly used in the USA, is technically incorrect, although the engines could be referred to as four-stroke-cycle engines. The classifications 'Four-Stroke' and 'Two-Stroke' are now becoming internationally accepted and these are the terms that will be used in this book.

Four-stroke engines

Four-stroke model engines are by no means a new innovation; a twin cylinder 'V' type, producing around 1.25 bhp, was being successfully operated in 1912 and the first official record for 'petrol flight' (powered by a four-stroke spark ignition engine) was set up in Britain in 1914. Professor Langley, who made the first outdoor flight with a steam driven model aircraft in 1896, is also reputed to have used a petrol engine in some of his experiments so we may be not too far short of the centennial anniversary of the model four-stroke engine!

The distinction between two-stroke and four-stroke engines (the principle remains the same whether spark, glow or compression ignition is involved) is that, to perform a full cycle of operations, i.e. changing the contents of the cylinders and effecting combustion, the four-stroke engine requires four 'strokes' of the piston and the two-stroke only two. By referring to the illustrations of 2-stroke and 4-stroke engines the differences of operation will become more apparent and the major design variation—the use of a cylinder head incorporating valves on the four-stroke engine—obvious.

Two-stroke operation

Although, for the purpose of illustration, the fuel/air mixture is shown entering the lower end of the cylinder, it is normal on model engines for the induction to be via a hollow crankshaft (front induction) or at the rear of the crankcase via a disc or drum valve (rear induction).

For a two-stroke engine, the crankcase must be hermetically sealed so that it can function as a pump, in conjunction with the piston (hence the reason why engines will not run satisfactorily with a loose backplate or front housing). With the piston at its highest point, the commencement of the first

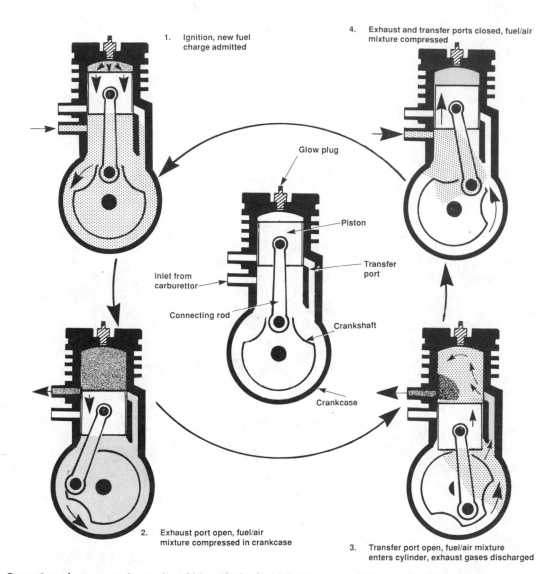

1. Ignition, new fuel charge admitted

4. Exhaust and transfer ports closed, fuel/air mixture compressed

Glow plug

Piston

Transfer port

Inlet from carburettor

Connecting rod

Crankshaft

Crankcase

2. Exhaust port open, fuel/air mixture compressed in crankcase

3. Transfer port open, fuel/air mixture enters cylinder, exhaust gases discharged

Operation of a two-stroke engine. Although the fuel inlet from the carburettor is shown on the side of the engine—for graphical purposes—it would normally enter from the hollow crankshaft (see page 10).

stroke, the compressed fuel/air mixture is ignited in the combustion chamber and the piston is forced downwards. During the descent the exhaust port is uncovered and the combustion gases are released. Further movement of the piston downwards coincides with the opening of the transfer port to allow the fuel/air mixture that has been compressed in the crankcase to flow into the cylinder above the piston. As the piston rises again, on the second stroke, it closes the inlet and exhaust ports and compresses the fuel/air mixture in the cylinder head; at the same time a suction is produced in the crankcase allowing a fresh fuel/air mixture to be drawn in.

By varying the bore/stroke ratio and the timing of the inlet and exhaust porting, the performance of the engine, and the speed (rpm) at which the engine will reach its maximum bhp, can be adjusted.

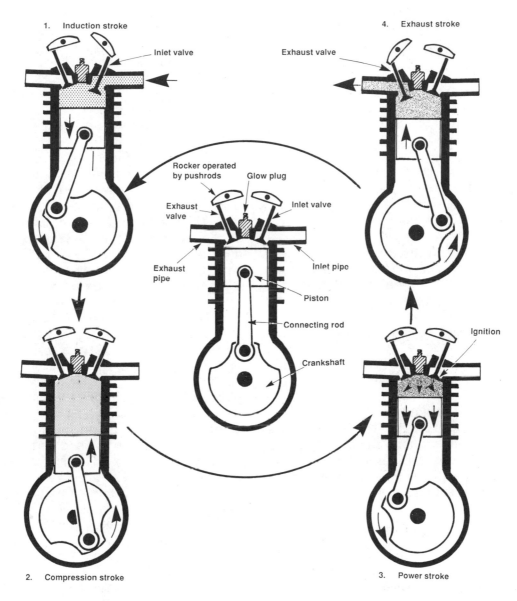

1. Induction stroke

Inlet valve

4. Exhaust stroke

Exhaust valve

Rocker operated by pushrods

Glow plug

Exhaust valve

Inlet valve

Exhaust pipe

Inlet pipe

Piston

Connecting rod

Crankshaft

Ignition

2. Compression stroke

3. Power stroke

Four-stroke operation

The above illustrates the operating principle of a single cylinder four-stroke engine with overhead poppet valves—usually pushrod operated from a camshaft.

The fuel/air mixture is metered by a carburettor of similar type to those used on two-stroke engines. It is common in model four-stroke engines to use a mixture of fuel and oil and rely on the natural dispersion of the oil for lubrication. Larger industrial four-stroke engines have a separate lubricating oil system.

No. 1—Induction Stroke. The descending piston draws into the cylinder a fresh fuel/air charge via the open inlet valve.

No. 2—Compression Stroke. Both valves are closed, and the ascending piston

17

compresses the gases in the combustion chamber.

No. 3—Power Stroke. Ignition of the gases creates pressure on the top of the piston and forces it downward. The valves remain closed.

No. 4—Exhaust Stroke. On the fourth, rising, stroke the outlet valve opens and the spent gases are discharged to atmosphere.

There are a number of different types of valves and methods of actuating them, some of which are discussed later, but the general operation of the engine remains the same. Twin cylinder, three cylinder—or any number of cylinder—engines are theoretically possible for four-stroke engines, the limiting practical factors being the complexity, and cost, of the engineering and the ability to control the fuel/air mixture to the separate cylinders.

Some examples, with simultaneous and alternate firing of the cylinders, are shown below; for manufacturing reasons the engines are mostly designed to feature simultaneous firing of the cylinders.

Carburettors

As the carburettor, on an R/C engine, is the only component that requires adjustment during the running of the engine it is important to understand the principles of operation and the practical results of making adjustments.

In its simplest form the carburettor is merely a metering and mixing device. Correctly set, it delivers a ratio of 12.5 parts of air to one part of petrol or 4.5 parts of air to one part of methanol, depending on the type of engine. Other components added to carburettors are used to alter the main and idle mixture, alter the delivery, pump raw fuel for starting or acceleration and restrict the delivery valve travel. G.B. Venturi (1746–1822), an Italian physicist, first developed the Venturi tube as a method of increasing the flow of liquids for added efficiency. By reducing the inside diameter of a tube at half the distance of its length and placing a jet orifice in the centre of the reduction, he found the suction pressure increased and created a more efficient flow. This is the basis of the modern-day carburettor.

The non-adjustable speed type of carburettor used on model engines con-

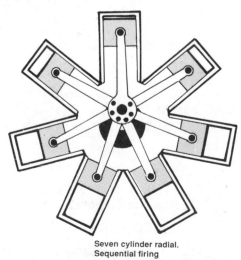

Seven cylinder radial.
Sequential firing

Layouts for twin cylinder and radial engines.

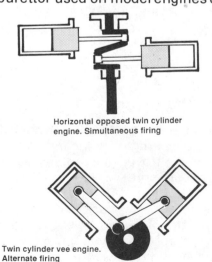

Horizontal opposed twin cylinder engine. Simultaneous firing

Twin cylinder vee engine.
Alternate firing

Intermediate type carburettor machined from aluminium alloy has rotating barrel, fuel nipple, adjustable throttle stop and secondary needle.

sists of a venturi, spraybar and needle valve or mixture adjusting needle. The most commonly used unit has a brass spraybar right across the venturi tube with a fuel inlet on one side and the needle adjust on the opposite side. No other adjustments are needed as the engine is run at constant speed. In the spraybar is a small hole or holes that are located centrally in the venturi passage. This is the fuel jet. If there is only one hole it is set to face downwards or towards the fuel timing valve or port. If there are two holes they are set to face across the venturi. As the engine turns and the valve or port opens, suction from the crankcase draws fuel from the jet. The needle or needle bar adjusts the amount of fuel to the volume of air to the proportion previously mentioned.

If the mixture adjustment is not correct and has too much fuel it is said to be a 'rich' mixture. Conversely, if there is too much air in the mixture it is said to be a 'lean' mixture as the fuel content is inadequate. The richness or leanness of the mixture always refers to the amount of FUEL—NOT AIR. While an engine will tolerate a mildly rich mixture and

will promote rapid wear, at least, or engine seizure at worst. As the engine gains forward motion, the venturi receives a certain amount of forced draught which will cause the mixture to lean out slightly. It is for this reason and sometimes benefit from this, a lean mix

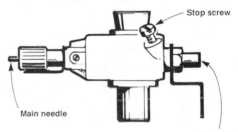

Stop screw

Main needle

Secondary needle

Rear view of intermediate type carburettor.

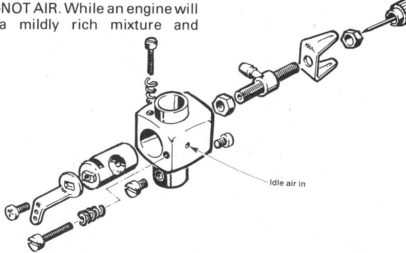

Idle air in

Exploded view of simple R/C carburettor showing the fuel adjusting needle, fuel nipple inlet, rotating barrel, servo arm connecting horn, air bleed adjustment and throttle stop screw.

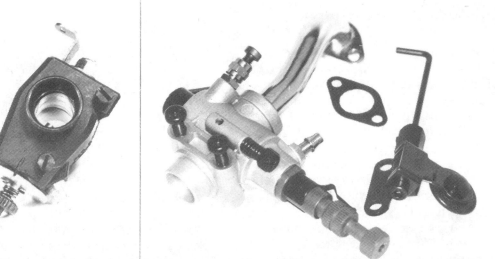

Perry carburettor, on left, has a brass knurled wheel for adjusting the mixture control. R/C carburettor on right is taken from a four-stroke engine. Note the inlet manifold and separate manual choke control—pulling the cranked rod will position the choke pad over the air intake.

the factor of reduced load (higher rpm in the air) that you are always advised to set a little on the rich side when the model is static. Once the needle is set it will only require minute adjustment for atmospheric changes—hot or cold days—so don't be a needle fiddler. The only other time you may need to adjust the mixture is if you change fuel, propeller or plug.

With models in the early days the only adjustment you had or needed over the carburettor once the model was released was the amount of fuel, as all control over engine speed ceased when it left your hands. With the advent of radio control, some refinement was desired to alter the engine speed for various manoeuvres, landing and take-off. Enter the variable speed carburettor. Different methods were tried such as rotating barrels, butterfly valves and sliding plates but the rotating drum is the most popular. There are several variations of the spraybar in this type of carburettor but the general principle is that the rotating barrel is drilled at one end for the main mixture control-needle valve, bored through the horizontal

centre for air passage and the actuating arm or throttle lever is attached to the end opposite the needle valve. Near the end with the lever, a slot is machined in the barrel and a small bolt threaded into the body of the carburettor locates in this slot. The purpose of the bolt is twofold. It retains the barrel in the carburettor body and can also be adjusted for the idle rpm by stopping the revolving travel of the barrel.

On a simple carburettor there is another bolt in the body retained by a compression spring. The end of this bolt interferes with a small hole in the front of the carburettor body. This is an air bleed idle mixture control. You will also find carburettors with a spraybar going right through the barrel and a slotted adjusting bolt inside the recessed throttle arm. This is also an idle adjustment but alters the fuel flow instead of the air as in the air bleed type. This type of carburettor is generally referred to as a compensating mixture control unit. Other variations will be a thin, knurled wheel, slotted disc or eccentric head bolt and pointer generally located adjacent to the main needle. These are all

Expansion chamber silencers are quite bulky but volume is part of the silencing requirement.

idle adjustments and require setting independently of the main fuel needle. The main mixture needle comes in a variety of forms according to the complexity of the carburettor and the choice of the manufacturer. Whatever type of needle is fitted, it is extremely important to keep certain rules in mind if you decide to extend the length of the operating section. This is often found necessary when the engine is cowled in or in a scale model where odd bits projecting from the cowl would ruin the aesthetics. The safest type of extension is tightly coiled spring and an easy supply of this can be purchased very cheaply at hardware stores. It is sold as expanding curtain rod!

As mentioned earlier, there are variations on the rotating barrel such as butterfly valves, sliding valves and horizontal travel barrel actions. One carburettor, the Webra Dynamix, even incorporates a form of accelerator pump to inject extra fuel when you 'open the tap'. Whatever the style, the basic principle is the same: mixture control and volume control for speed variation.

Silencers

Silencers, also known as mufflers in some countries, are an accepted part of virtually all model engines, even the quieter-operating four-stroke motors. Although silencers were first introduced purely to reduce the noise levels, the manufacturers realised that the loss of performance resulting from fitting the silencers might not be acceptable. They therefore set about changing the design of engine bore/stroke ratios, porting methods and silencer designs to keep the performance losses to a minimum. Indeed, they were so successful with the tuned pipe system of silencers that the noise levels were reduced and performance was actually *increased*.

Tuned pipe silencers tend to be

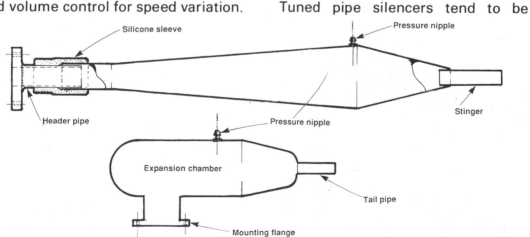

Tuned pipe silencers, top, have to be designed and adjusted to give maximum performance. Expansion silencers are strictly non-critical but cause some power loss.

Engines designed for racing models, such as pylon racers, normally have rear exhaust positions so that the tuned pipe silencers are easier to fit and adjust. Power increases are possible with tuned pipe silencers.

restricted to competition type models, notably aerobatic and pylon models, as they are more difficult to install and require adjusting to obtain maximum performance.

Sports engines are normally fitted with an 'expansion chamber' style silencer. These are designed to allow the exhaust gases to expand and cool before leaving the tail pipe. How effective the silencer is will depend on the volume of the chamber/s, how smooth are the transition bends from the exhaust outlet of the engine to the chamber, how many exhaust baffles are fitted and the total mass of the silencer. Silencer design is, or should be, as important as the engine design and manufacturers are becoming increasingly aware of this fact.

If the exhaust gases can't expand and get away quickly they can cause a back pressure which will rapidly overheat the engine. Manufacturers are aware of this problem; it should be borne in mind by modellers fabricating their own silencers for models. There is a great risk when fitting an own-design silencer to a scale model of making the expansion chamber too small and having a tortuous route for the exhaust manifold. All this is conducive to overheating of the engine and this is often augmented by poor cooling arrangements in cowled engines—a recipe for disaster.

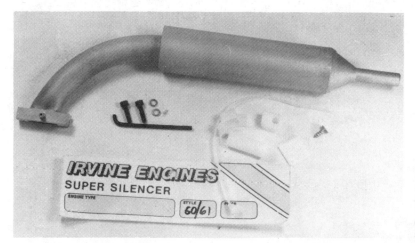

So called 'Super Silencers' are a mixture of expansion and tuned pipe silencers. Power losses, if any, will be minimal with this style of silencer.

Chapter 3
After-purchase
preparation and running in

PERHAPS IT is because we live in an 'instant' world where there is so little time to do everything we should do—or want to do—that we try to take short cuts. How often do you read the operating manual of a new car before you sit in it and drive off? Have you really read the instruction manual of your fully automatic camera? After all, if it *is* fully automatic you shouldn't need to bother. Model engines, in comparison with some of the more sophisticated pieces of machinery, are relatively simple, so surely we don't need to worry about that leaflet stuffed in the box with the new engine? That is just for the idiots of this world, *we* were not born yesterday, *we* know that you have to run in any engine and make sure that it is not 'raced' immediately and the fuel kept rather rich.

So, we bolt our gleaming piece of metal to the bench, fire it up, admire the workmanship and simple operation, give it two or three runs and then retire into the house for dinner. Feeling rather satisfied and having fed the inner man we might as well have a look through those bits of paper in the engine. 'Running In. This engine is fitted with a high technology super silicone chrome deposited finish to the piston and liner and extensive damage will be caused to

the engine unless the operating instructions are followed precisely'—or words to that effect. My heavens, not only have we probably ruined the engine but we have almost certainly made the guarantee null and void also. We had forgotten about the guarantee, hadn't we?

Manufacturers go to a lot of trouble these days to write thorough instructions regarding their products. You ignore them at your peril. Study (not just read, but STUDY) them before you so much as lay a finger on the engine.

To strip or not

You will *not* find in the instructions a suggestion that you dismantle any part of the engine before you run it. Most probably the instructions will be exactly opposite and they will be warning you away from ever dismantling the engine and encouraging modellers to return the engine to servicing agents if any work is required. For the non-mechanical/technical modeller this is sound advice as it is easy to cause a great deal of damage to the engine by taking it apart in the wrong way or with the wrong tools. However, there are plenty of modellers with sufficient skills to be able to strip an engine, carry out the necessary servicing or replacement work, and assemble it again, without fear of destroying the unit. But what about the pre-run situation?

Very few engine manufacturers run all their engines before they leave the factory. This time-consuming operation is usually confined to manufacturers of diesel engines, where knowledge of the operating settings of the compression screw and needle valve is important for the purchaser. Skilled staff are employed in the assembly of model engines, but they are not modellers, and it is possible for a piece of swarf (metal turning) to be left inside the engine during the assembly. Although this is not a common occurrence, many modellers consider it worthwhile to remove the backplate of the engine to make a visual inspection for any 'foreign bodies'. After removal of the backplate—and, carefully, the gasket—the glow plug is also removed. Cellulose thinners, or cellulose cleaning liquid, is poured through the plug hole and the engine given a thorough shake to see if any metal slivers are deposited in the lower part of the crankcase. The chances are that the engine will be clean but, if not, remove the loose articles, rinse through again and lightly oil before refitting the backplate. Remember to tighten the backplate bolts in diagonally opposite sequences as is good engineering practice. If the thought of partially dismembering a new engine horrifies you, don't worry, just leave things well alone. With small pieces of aluminium loose in the engine the worst that may happen is for the glowplug elements to fail on one or two plugs as small pieces of the debris impinge on the spiral-wound plug element.

How much running-in an engine will require will depend on the type of engine and the materials used in manufacture. A lapped piston motor, i.e. a piston not fitted with rings of any type, will require a lot of running-in time as the area of contact surfaces is considerable and these all have to be mated together. Ringed piston engines of the conventional type will not need as long a running-in period as the lapped piston type, but still an hour or so to allow the parts to 'bed in'. Modern ABC and AAC engines require a minimum of running-in but remember that it is also necessary to bed-in other moving components (crankshaft bearings, little and big con-rod end bearings etc.) and that you should take care with any engine in the early part of its life.

Engines of the same manufacture and type will also vary in the amount of running-in they require. Some will be 'tight' when they leave the assembly line, others will free when they are turned over by hand. It is vital to remember that an engine can be ruined in a minute or two by careless operation initially and by setting the fuel supply too lean. The converse is also true; if you take time to run in a new engine with tender loving care it will repay you time and again. Model engines are rather like beautiful women; delightful to look at but of far more value if treated with respect and fully understood. Taking the time to find out what makes an engine 'tick' will give an insight to the methods of operation and assist when it comes to maintenance and servicing.

Ground or air testing

Having read the instructions and inspected and cleaned the engine we are ready for the big moment. Incidentally, if we do find anything obviously wrong with the engine it must be returned to the retailer, servicing agent or manufacture—as stated in the guarantee.

Can we carry out the running-in operations with the engine fitted to the model? We can, but there are disadvantages. With modern engines requiring only short run-in periods this operation can be carried out in the air. We must, however, ensure that the engine is not set too lean or, by the time we have heard the distress of the engine and throttled back, it may have already caused damage to the engine. It is not good policy to continue a long process of running-in on an engine that is fitted to the model being held near the ground. Loose dirt and debris will be picked up by the propeller and there is a strong risk of it being ingested by the air intake. In all circumstances, including the ones that require little running-in, it is better to carry out these operations with the engine fitted to a bench. This gives immediate access to the engine, allowing you to adjust the carburettor, or stop the engine, should it be needed. If you do not have facilities at home to run engines, then you can rig up a stand at the flying field for the engine, or for the model and engine, at a reasonable distance from the ground. Do not site your stand too close to the model flying area—there is nothing more annoying than having an engine screaming away in your ear for prolonged periods.

If you consider that you are going to stay with this hobby for some time you will, no doubt, purchase more engines in time—it becomes habit-forming—in which case, purchase an engine test stand. There are some excellent ones on the market with the capacity to hold from the smallest beam mount engine to a .90 (15 cc) and they are surprisingly inexpensive. Many times you will want to run an engine for some reason or other and it is so simple to just clamp it in the test stand without the bother of making up a wood mount and finding the correct bolts for the job. If your pocket doesn't run that deep at present then you can mount the engine on a flat

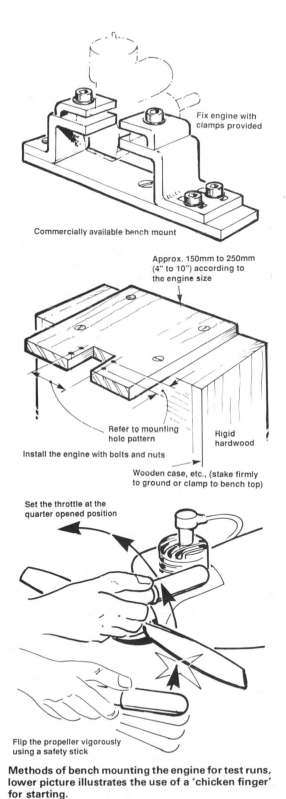

Fix engine with clamps provided

Commercially available bench mount

Approx. 150mm to 250mm (4" to 10") according to the engine size

Refer to mounting hole pattern

Rigid hardwood

Install the engine with bolts and nuts

Wooden case, etc., (stake firmly to ground or clamp to bench top)

Set the throttle at the quarter opened position

Flip the propeller vigorously using a safety stick

Methods of bench mounting the engine for test runs, lower picture illustrates the use of a 'chicken finger' for starting.

Engine test stands will hold small and moderate sized engines securely. Larger engines i.e. '45' and upwards, should be bolted in position.

Engine test stands will hold small and moderate sized engines securely. Larger engines i.e. '45' and upwards, should be bolted in position.

slab of wood. Don't be tempted to use the first piece of wood that comes to hand—it needs to be hard, absolutely flat and not inclined to split.

The mount is set up with provision for a tank to be held with rubber bands and a bracket with a threaded wire and clevis for the throttle, and the bolts are left with each mount. Before I forget—under no circumstances should you ever clamp an engine in a vice. To do this will distort the crankcase and the grip on the narrow edge of the lug is of such a small area that the engine could easily slip out while running. You can use plain softwood board for mounting an engine, but plywood or blockboard are more suitable as they tend to split or compress less than softwood. Cut out one end of the board to fit the engine and drill the holes for the mounting bolts. Screw on a couple of small blocks for supporting the throttle operating wire and a couple of cup hooks for the fuel tank retaining rubber bands. The mounting board may either be held in the jaws of a large vice (allowing the engine to project clear of the surrounding bench) or, preferably, screwed down to a solid bench or suitable structure.

The engine is now mounted, the throttle connected to the wire control, the fuel tank is full and connected to the carburettor. Tighten the propeller on the engine so that, viewed from the front, it is in a '20 minutes-to-two o'clock' position as it just comes up against compression.

Everything else is tight or secure, no loose rag near the prop or items on the bench to blow over in prop wash and you should be wearing safety glasses.

Starting

You can go three ways in starting the engine: finger, in which case a rubber finger protector is advisable, 'chicken stick', a wooden handle with a rubber end to flick the prop, or electric starter. The choice is yours but remember that both the chicken stick and the electric starter do not give you a feel of the engine so make sure it is not flooded (hydraulic lock) as damage could occur if the engine is forced over under these conditions. With the throttle fully open and the main needle screwed out four turns, place your index finger firmly over the air intake and turn over the prop slowly until the fuel comes up the tube to the carburettor nipple. When the fuel is at this position, turn the prop again

Hand operated 'chicken finger' and motorised starter.

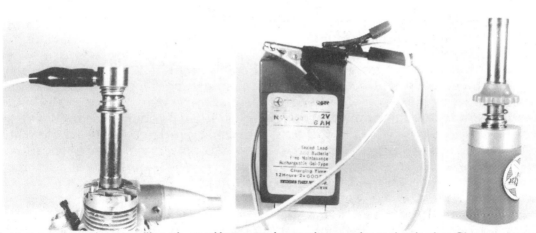

To start any glo-engine you will need a good battery and a sound connection to the glo plug. Glo connector on left is particularly suited to cowled-in engines. Rechargeable 2 volt batteries (around 5 to 7AH) are used for the power source, unless a 1.5 volt plug is being used. Right hand glo plug energiser has a built in nickel cadmium rechargeable cell attached.

with your finger still on the air intake twice for a small engine up to 3 cc, four times for 4-7 cc and six times for 7-10 cc. Flick the prop three or four times smartly before connecting the battery. This gets the fuel mix into the combustion area. Connect up the battery, hold one blade of the prop *firmly* and turn the engine over slowly. You should feel a 'bump' or slight resistance as the engine goes over compression. This indicates that the fuel is in the chamber and the engine is ready to start. If you do not feel a 'bump' on the third turn, disconnect the plug and flick the prop another three or four times and try again. If still no 'bump', give the engine another choke, three flicks and try again. If still no response, check the plug is glowing bright orange. When you feel the 'bump', flick the engine smartly and it should start on first or second flick. There are two schools of thought on the starting position of the throttle—some say full throttle—others go for fast idle. I prefer fast idle—throttle about one-third open and I don't have any starting problems at this. At one-third throttle, the engine is under the influence of the main needle—we can sort out the idle tuning later. The engine will be running

quite rich, but should continue to run when the plug lead is disconnected. If not, it may indicate that the plug is too cold. Now we can see the reason for opening the needle four turns before starting. The first run of the engine is really rich with loads of oil going through. If an engine is started lean, screams away and dies soon after, chances are that you have worn out quite a few hours of use in those few seconds. Open the throttle slowly and wind the needle in also slowly to the rpm recommended in the instruction sheet. If you don't have a tachometer (revolution counter) then wind the needle

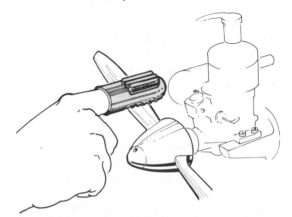

Use a finger guard, or thick glove, if you are starting by hand—even small engines can bite.

until you hear the engine just breaking in and out of lean two-stroke running. This is indicated by a high pitch sound which is very smooth in note. Open the throttle back out about four or five clicks—about 1/8th of a turn—to rich running and follow the running-in procedure.

When you have finished running the engine to the point where it is ready for use, open the throttle right up and pull the fuel line off the carburettor. By doing this you will run the engine dry of fuel but, by this time, all the internal components will be well coated with oil so the brief lean run will do no harm. Fuel left in an engine can cause corrosion so the less left inside the better. Wipe the outside of the engine with a clean cloth, squirt five or six drops of oil into the exhaust port or, if you are leaving the muffler on, remove the plug and drop the oil through the plug hole. Put a similar amount into the carburettor and turn the engine over four or five times to distribute the oil. Remove the prop, check the outside of the engine for problems or loose bolts—rectify if necessary—and place it in a sturdy plastic bag—sealed—ready to use in your model. When you go to the field for the inaugural flight, you should not have any problems with the engine: use the same starting procedure for an instant start and keep it slightly rich for the first few tanks of fuel.

A few DON'TS for running a new engine

Don't run the engine for a prolonged period in a model on the ground. To do this will cause considerable wear due to the grit blown up by the prop into the carburettor. The liner will varnish up due to the prolonged running at rich mixture and static load and it is a waste of fuel.

Don't run a high percentage of nitro-methane in the fuel during running in. The extra combustion load on the new engine from a high nitro fuel could cause damage. Increase the nitro content to that recommended by the manufacturer as the engine becomes well run in. Don't overload a new engine with a large prop. It will cause strain and overheat the engine. An engine needs to run lightly loaded during the running in period.

Don't let 'seasoned' modellers talk you out of running-in the engine if the manufacturer indicates it is needed. For engines that need it, the run-in period is the most important part of its life. A well run-in engine will give many hours of trouble free use and be a source of enjoyment in your modelling. It is nice to be able to say that your engine has been flying models for you for three or four years without a hint of trouble. THAT engine was run in correctly.

Four-stroke engines

Although starting techniques are similar for all types of engines there are several significant differences between starting two and four-stroke engines. At the risk of repeating some of the previous description, here are some methods for getting the latter engines going.

Four-strokes like a rich fuel mixture for starting and failure to start is more often attributable to too little fuel being present in the combustion chamber than too much—another reason for having a glow plug with a really healthy glow. Increasingly, manufacturers are fitting manually operated chokes to engines as carburettors are frequently situated at the rear of the engine and it is not always easy to position the finger over the air intake to suck the fuel into the carburettor.

1. Open up the main needle valve

between ½ and 1½ turns beyond the normal running position—the amount will vary from engine to engine.

2. Check that the fuel is reaching the carburettor and choke the engine by turning the propeller over four or five turns with the air inlet to the carburettor blocked off.

3. Prime the cylinder head, i.e. squirt a few drops of neat fuel through the exhaust pipe with the exhaust valve open—this is easy to see with open valves, with enclosed rockers and pushrods the propeller must be turned over a couple of times, with the prime in, to make sure the fuel enters the combustion chamber. Note: It may be inconvenient to introduce a prime with the exhaust pipe in certain positions and in these instances you will have to rely on choking alone. Most engines will respond to this, although starting may not be quite so instantaneous.

4. Turn the propeller over by hand for two full revolutions to make sure that the combustion chamber is not over-primed—flooding can cause an hydraulic lock and damage to the valve gear. If it is intended to use an electric starter, the engine should always be 'flicked' over by hand before applying the starter to reduce the risk of 'hydraulicing'; *omit* the additional priming into the exhaust pipe when a starter is used.

5. Connect the battery lead to the glow plug and allow a few seconds for it to heat up thoroughly. Open up the throttle fully.

6. Grasp one blade of the propeller firmly and turn through two revolutions. There should be a noticeable 'kick' as the piston reaches top dead centre on the firing stroke—a sure

Overhead rotary valve is used on this four-stroke engine instead of the more common poppet valves.

sign that there is fuel present and the glow plug is 'live'. Providing that you hold the propeller firmly and revolve it slowly there is no risk of the engine 'biting' you.

7. The next action will depend on the specific engine you are starting. Some respond best to flicking in the conventional manner, i.e. a sharp flick in an anti-clockwise direction, but others respond more readily to a backwards (clockwise) bounce-flick technique. The latter technique tends to be more successful with engines featuring relatively high compression ratios, e.g. the O.S.FS60.

One reason for favouring the clockwise swing of the propeller (it is a routine quickly learned) is the full fuel charge in the combustion chamber and the hot plug; flicking for normal rotation may cause a backfire. Whichever direction of flicking you find gives the best results it is always wise to use a finger protector. Never consider the use of rubber finger guards as effeminate since any engine can 'bite' and four-stroke engines are no exception! The use of 'chicken sticks' is less advisable as they do not allow any direct feel of the condition of the engine.

8. When the engine is running, slowly close the needle valve until the

engine starts to lean out. Because the sound of a four-stroke is significantly different from a two-stroke it will take a bit of experiment before you become attuned to finding the optimum setting. The engine will cut quite rapidly if the needle valve is closed down too far but neither is the needle setting immediately adjacent to the 'cut-out' the correct one. Open up beyond the minimum lean setting and you should be able to hear to a noticeable, if slight, speed increase. A little on the rich side is preferable to a lean setting, the more so during running in.

9. Remove the glowplug lead. Any appreciable drop in rpm with the battery disconnected suggests that that the fuel/glow plug combination is incorrect, although a small loss of power may be inevitable until the engine is fully run in.

Diesel engines

A different technique is also needed for starting and adjusting diesel engines. Because the diesel relies on compression ignition the flick of the propeller, as stated in Chapter 1, has to be rapid—it is no good gently flicking over the propeller; the engine will either not fire or it will backfire and rap you on the finger. Use of an electric starter is definitely *not* recommended for diesel engines. Being of small capacities the diesel can easily be damaged by over-compressing or flooding the engine and applying a powerful electric starter. It is necessary to get the feel of the state of the diesel as the propeller is flicked over, i.e. if it has too much fuel, or is undercompressed, etc. This is something which will only be experienced by hand starting the engine.

Where no silencer is fitted, squirt a couple of drops of fuel onto the crown of the piston, through the exhaust ports. *Turn* the propeller over, if there is any major resistance reduce the compression by a quarter of a turn (anticlockwise viewed from above). Check that the fuel is through to the carburettor and flick the engine smartly over. If there is only slight resistance, but the engine doesn't fire, keep flicking away and *increasing* the compression until the engine does fire. You may find that you have to further increase the compression to keep the engine running, but at the sound of the engine running 'hard' reduce the compression immediately. With the engine running steadily experiment with the needle valve to obtain the fastest running and then richen the mixture again slightly. After the engine has been running for a minute or two you may find that you have to slacken off the compression screw due to engine warming up— particularly with a new engine.

Describing, in writing, the starting and setting of a diesel always sounds a traumatic business. In reality, it is nowhere near as difficult to get used to operating a diesel as might be thought, but there is a knack to be learned and some modellers seem to find it a difficult skill to master.

Chapter 4
Installing and operating the engine in a model

MOUNTING THE engine in your model is every bit as important as, say, setting the wing square with the tail surfaces. An incorrectly set-up engine can cause vibration and/or odd flying characteristics. Few modellers bother to trim the engine mounting on a new model. They just keep compensating with elevator or rudder at each change of engine speed.

My favourite method of engine mounting is to use hardwood rails as far apart as possible to form a crutch for the front of the fuselage. There are many advantages in using this system, some being that it makes a good, solid front end for the model, it provides a space for the tank and a platform for the throttle cable, cowl mounting is easier and no bolt ends protruding into the tank area; there are also easy mounting for front nose gear and, most important, a stable platform for the engine.

The engine is mounted on a Paxolin or ply plate (or plates) and these plates are screwed or bolted to the rails. The engine is firmly mounted, vibration is reduced, no pressure is exerted on the crankcase due to uneven bedding surfaces, thrustline adjustments are simple (by moving the plate) and engine replacement is a five-minute job. (If you like to experiment with different en-gines in a particular model, make several blank mounting plates and drill them all the same for the rail mounting holes. It is then only a matter of making a cut-out for the engine, mounting it on the plate and screwing the plate to the rails). Another bonus is that in the event of a 'ploughman's landing' the engine plate absorbs most of the impact and is, quite often, the only damaged part. If you use plywood for the plate, use only marine grade multi-ply as 'cupboard' ply is too soft and 'squashy'.

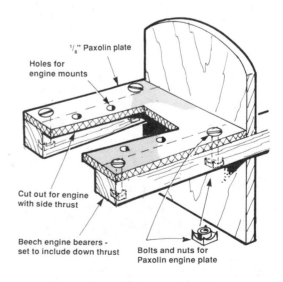

Paxolin plate engine mounting.

Labels in figure: $\frac{1}{8}$" Paxolin plate; Holes for engine mounts; Cut out for engine with side thrust; Beech engine bearers - set to include down thrust; Bolts and nuts for Paxolin engine plate.

You don't have to go overboard on strength as ¼in. ply is quite adequate for the largest of true model engines. You can also use aluminium for the plate, but watch the thickness. Up to a .30 engine you could use $\frac{1}{16}$in., .30 to .60 use $\frac{1}{8}$in. and up to .90 use $\frac{3}{16}$in. Anything larger in two-stroke would need ¼in. Drill all holes tight clearance for the bolts and maintain the bolt tightness with spring washers, locknuts or Nyloc nuts.

If I use aluminium, I prefer to use Allen head or cheesehead bolts and counterbore the plate enough to allow the heads to locate in the aluminium. If you use a single plate with a cut-out for the engine, make sure the back corners of the cut-out are radiused. All these precautions are necessary as aluminium fatigues quickly when subjected to vibration and cracks occur at sharp corners and loose fitted bolt holes.

Radial mounts

If you choose to use these ready-made mounts there are several points to consider. First, are the mounting rails true and square to the wall mount? Lay a

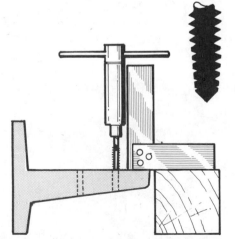

Mark out the mounting hole positions carefully on the engine mount. Drill pilot holes and then tap for engine bolts—ensure verticality.

steel rule or metal straight-edge across the rails and check for light under the edge of the rule. If the light appears as a wedge it means that the mounts are not true and will need resurfacing with a file or, preferably, on a milling machine.

If the rails are not square to the mounting plate you will have to machine this surface or compensate when mounting. Most of these types of mounts on the market are of superb quality, but I have seen some that leave a lot to be desired. The few pennies you save on buying the 'cheapies' will be offset by the time required to correct bad workmanship. If the faults aren't corrected the crankcase of your engine could be distorted and overload the bearings or break off a mounting lug.

Most mounts have a tapered underside to the mounting rails which makes them unsuitable for through bolting—that is, using bolts with nuts. This can be overcome by spot-facing the drilled hole on the tapered side. If you don't have a spot-facing drill on hand, countersink the hole and then square off the tapered hole with a flat end drill. The ideal method for mounting an engine on these mounts is to tap a thread for the bolts in the rails. Spot-face the underside and secure the bolts with a locknut. Always put the bolts down through the engine lugs when mounting as this will, at least, keep the engine in place, albeit shakily, if the nut vibrates off. If you bring the bolt up from underneath it can drop out and the engine has no security at all.

Accurate drilling of the holes so they match the holes in the engine lugs is important. Obtain a short length of steel rod of a size that fits neatly through the holes in the mounting lugs of your engine. Cut off a piece about 1 in. long and mount in your lathe or drill chuck. Truly sharpen the point at an angle of about 45°. Cut the pointed end off about

¼ in. long overall. Engineering modellers will know how to use heat treatable steel or will case-harden mild steel. Standard modellers, without these facilities, can heat the pin to red heat and leave it in some sugar until cool. This will harden the steel suitably for the job. Sit the engine in position on the mount and fit the pin in either of the front mounting holes, point down. Give it a tap with something hard and then remove the engine; you should have a centre dot on the mount. Drill for tapping size, spot-face bottom edge and tap thread. Make sure you drill the hole at 90° both ways to the bearer, otherwise the bolt will be at an angle and this is a sure way of setting up a bolt to snap under the strain of vibration.

Set the engine back and screw in the one bolt. Adjust your engine now for any side thrust if desired and 'pin-point' the other front hole. Repeat the first operation.

Remount the engine and bolt firmly with the two front bolts. Pin both the rear holes now, drill and tap using a try-square. The little extra trouble will pay for itself in an accurate mounting job and you won't have to elongate the holes in the engine beams.

Mounting the mount

From a cleaned and 'opened out' tin can cut a piece the same shape and size as the firewall mounting plate of the engine mount unit (square or round). Lightly glue the tinplate to the rear of the mount with just a couple of dabs of acetate glue (balsa cement). Set the mount on the firewall in the position required with modelling clay and drill one hole through the tin and the

Resilient mounting for engines, to reduce vibration effects and transmitted sound, are being used increasingly. Large rubber grommets provide isolation of mount in this instance.

firewall. Insert a bolt to locate the hole. Drill another hole and insert another bolt. Drill the remaining two holes. Mark the tinplate, mount and firewall with a felt pen for location purposes. Remove the mount and cut the tinplate off the back with a sharp knife. Clean off the glue dabs.

Sit the tinplate back on the mount and drop in the four bolts you are going to use for the mounting. The heads of the bolts will be on the tinplate. NEATLY solder the heads to the plate (no ugly big blobs, please). Clean off flux residue. Place this 'bolt mount' into the fuel tank bay and insert the bolts into the holes in the firewall. Fit the mount and secure with Nyloc nuts or plain nuts and shakeproof washers. A simple, secure job that is efficient and virtually maintenance free.

Direct beam mounting

Direct mounting on timber beams is not so popular with R/C fliers due to tank placement problems, but it is suitable for some models. Make sure the timber used is straight, close grain hardwood. The hardwood strips sold in model shops are far superior to a bit of scrap wood saved from the fire kindling. Always sand the wood immediately

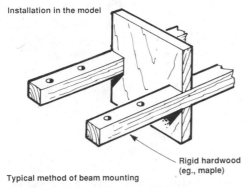

Installation in the model

Rigid hardwood
(eg., maple)

Typical method of beam mounting

Simple hardwood beam engine mount.

prior to glueing as timber oxidises and leaches resinous oils when left after machining and this inhibits glue adhesion. Drill these mounts using the method described for radial mounts, but check for tightness after the first two or three flights as the wood will compress a little, leaving the bolts loose.

There are other methods of engine mounting using a variety of materials that are occasionally employed but, whatever method you use, make it secure, true and keep the bolts tight.

Fuel tanks

The design of R/C fuel tanks (clunk tanks) has not changed to any great degree since an enterprising American modeller realised the potential of a polythene bottle with a rubber bung in the neck. So, if they are so easy to use and have been in use for so long, why do so many modellers seem to have problems with them? Simply because they do not follow the basic requirement for a good tank and plumbing arrangement. So let's start by considering a few of these basics before going on to the actual installation.

1. Fuel tubing. You must use the correct type of fuel tubing for the engine being used and it should be of the best quality available. For spark ignition (petrol) engines use only neoprene or plastic tubing sold by automotive stores for this purpose. Neoprene is also the right material for diesels, but there are other plastics that are suitable and sold specifically for diesel engines. Glow engines require silicone tubing for the plumbing; use a grade where the wall thickness is such that it will not easily collapse when taken round a bend. If there is a severe radius bend to negotiate you can insert a spring (from a cigarette lighter or similar) in the tubing; this will prevent the tube kinking.

2. Tank size. Don't use an excessively large tank in a model. Not only will this increase the overall weight of the model (and give larger changes of c.g. positions) but it will increase

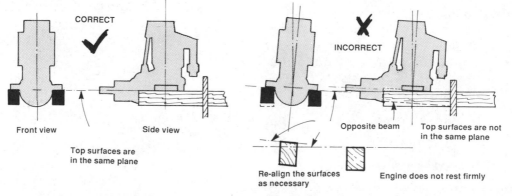

CORRECT

Front view Side view

Top surfaces are
in the same plane

INCORRECT

Opposite beam Top surfaces are not
in the same plane

Re-align the surfaces
as necessary

Engine does not rest firmly

Always check for 'squareness' of bearers before mounting engine.

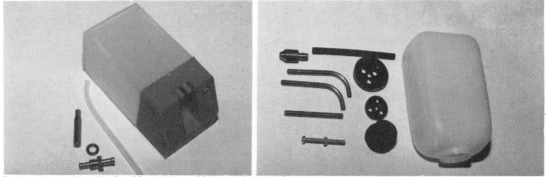

Fuel tanks can be obtained in square, oblong and round formats and various combinations of shapes. Virtually all tanks operate on the 'clunk' pick-up system, whereby a weighted fuel pick-up is attached to a flexible pipe inside the tank. The freely moving 'clunk' will allow fuel to be drawn from the tank with the model in most attitudes.

the chances of fuel surges. Our commercial fuel tanks do not have baffles fitted and the fuel in the tank can 'slop' around rapidly, giving conditions for fuel surging if the tank is over-large.

3. Filters. There is controversy regarding the fitting of fuel filters in the line between the fuel tank and the carburettor. However, there is no controversy regarding the need to filter the fuel as it is being put *into* the fuel tank. In fact, the more it is filtered at this stage the better. If you do wish to install an inline filter it should be positioned adjacent to the carburettor with filling of the tank (for a two pipe tank system) always from the rear of the filter. Two-piece filters, which can be taken apart for cleaning, can be a source of air leakage— and intermittent engine running— check that they are tightened and leak-proof.

4. Metal fuel tubes. When you fit dry silicone tubing to *dry* metal tubing you will find that it will continue to hold there. With fuel-wet tubing the silicone will attempt to shrink off the metal tubing. A cure for this problem, with brass tubing, is to wrap around a piece of tinned copper wire and to solder it into place, forming a nipple on the end of the tubing. The shape

is similar to the nipple turned into the end of the fuel intake on the engine carburettor.

Fuel tank installation

Fuel tanks are often fitted and forgotten! This being the case we must be sure to put the tank in the correct position and have the plumbing as reliable as possible. Even so, faults can occur and it must be feasible to gain access to the fuel tank in an emergency.

All models should be built with prime importance given to tank position. Right from the start, let us set the rules. The tank is positioned as close to the firewall as possible. The measured centre-line of the tank—not the outlet pipe—is set ¼in. to ⅜in. below the needle valve of the engine. Of course, a fuel pump negates this rule. The tank is to be set in soft foam to stop the fuel from frothing with the engine vibration. This little job is often neglected and accounts for a high number of tuning problems. It is impossible to set the tune on an engine if the fuel is frothing, due to the constant changing air fuel ratio as more air is introduced from the air bubbles in the fuel. Make sure the tank is completely isolated from any solid item in contact with the airframe as vibration is easily transmitted.

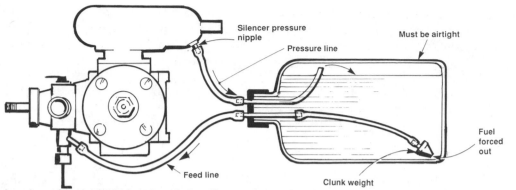

A plan view of a typical fuel tank and plumbing arrangement. With this two pipe system the tank is filled through the feed line removed from the carburettor nipple.

The best way is to wrap the tank lengthways in foam and secure the wrap with masking tape. Put a block of foam against the rear of the firewall, position tank against this block and fill space between the end of the tank and the bulkhead. If there is any space left between the tank and the fuselage sides, fill with scrap foam to keep the tank in position. It is not good practice to build the tank into your model due to the fact that the more you enclose it the more chance there is of something going wrong, necessitating its removal on the field.

The metal tubes in the tank neck can be a source of problems if not cut correctly. It is extremely difficult to de-burr the cut ends of these tubes without leaving a sharp edge. Sharp edges put nasty little nicks in fuel tube and the resultant tuning problems are blamed on the engine!

The best way is to use a tubing cutter. These are available for modellers' use in small sizes and are in the form of a vee-block with an adjustable wheel.

When you cut tubing with this tool, the end of the tube is swaged inwards to give a slightly rounded end to the tube and no burr. While you are waiting to purchase yours, you can do a fair job with a long-blade modelling knife. Lay the tube on a hard surface, place the knife edge where you want the cut and roll the tube with the knife. Go steady at first to make a single line around the tube, keep the blade at 90° to the tubing. Apply moderate pressure and continue rolling.

You will notice the tube is rolling inwards with the cut until the tube parts. A very light rub with a piece of glass will remove any burr formed. Do not use garnet or similar paper for deburring as you can never be sure that you do not leave a bit of grit in the tube.

I only use two tubes in the tank—one for engine supply and tank filling and the other for muffler pressure and overflow. A separate tube for filling can be a nuisance, as it can cause engine flooding when filling and is another area to worry about air leaks.

Another area of concern is the setting-up of the clunk and the overflow, which has to be set close to the inside front of the tank at the highest point. Some of the new tanks on the market now have a little blister on top of the tank for this purpose. The generally accepted practice for the setting-up of the clunk is to fix a weight on the end of a flexible tube to follow the fuel around the tank.

The fact of the matter is that the fuel does not move very much at all in the tank when the model is moving. Nature's law of force and motion keeps the fuel piled up against the rear wall of the tank for almost all movements of the model.

A length of copper tube attached to the neck tube with a silicone tube universal joint is quite adequate. Copper, because of its weight, is recommended rather than aluminium or brass.

If your clunk is close to the rear wall, or the connection to it is flexible enough for it to turn around and touch the side wall, the suction of the engine will make it stick to the wall. When this occurs, the engine starts to die, suction is reduced and the engine picks up again. When maximum suction is again reached you go through the whole cycle again.

Purpose-made tanks

It is possible to make fuel tanks from tin plate—or even plywood—for special installations, mainly relating to scale models. For trainer and sports models, however, it should be possible to select a suitable commercial tank from one of the many on sale. They come in round, oblong and oval shapes!

Operating the engine in the model

Although the engine may have been run in before fitting in the model you will need to make final adjustments for actual flying conditions. Assuming that the plumbing is right, you have the correct plug and propeller fitted and you are using the prescribed fuel, it should be only the carburettor that requires final adjustment. If you are taking this opportunity to change from a running-in fuel, with more oil, to a standard fuel, you will certainly need to make adjustments to the carb, possibly a plug type change also. Once the carburettor needle settings are determined you should only need to adjust *slightly* in the future to compensate for weather conditions.

Any major change of needle settings *definitely* indicates some other problem.

On the first flight I would advise that you open the needle ¼ turn richer and see how the model and engine behave in the air. It is much better to have a slightly rich first flight than to have the engine unload and run lean. Remember—winding in = lean mixture, winding out = rich mixture. A lean mixture is your enemy. Avoid it!

Right, we have the top end tuned, now for the idle. Close the barrel down until the engine is running at about 2,500 to 3,000 rpm and screw the throttle stop bolt (incorrectly called a screw) down until it holds the barrel in this position. If the engine gains rpm and stops, the idle mixture is too lean—if the rpm die down and the engine stops it is too rich. If you have an air bleed carb.—hole in front, spring loaded bolt—you will have to adjust the mixture with this bolt. Screwing in gives a rich mixture and screwing out gives a lean mixture. If your carburettor has the mixture control in the end of the barrel with the throttle arm you will have to adjust this and *generally* turning clockwise is lean and vice versa. On carburettors with a knurled wheel or slotted disc you will often find a plus (+) and minus (−) sign on the carburettor body. Turning in the direction of the plus sign richens the mixture. In any case, check the instruction leaflet for precise operation of this control. Once you have tuned the idle mixture your engine should hold the idle r.p.m. for at least several minutes or more and gain high r.p.m. when you open the throttle. If the engine stops on transition—changing from low to high r.p.m.—it could indicate that you have set the idle too low or your plug is unsuitable (refer to fault-finding section). On the occasional carb, you will find a mid-range tuning adjustment. As these extra adjustments are rare it is best to refer to the instruction manual for precise operation. Generally, the engine is tuned correctly at both ends of the scale, the throttle is turned to mid-range r.p.m., checked with a tachometer ('rev' counter) and the adjustment made to obtain even running. Due to the simplicity (thankfully) of the carburettors used on model engines, it is not generally possible to obtain 100% perfect tune throughout the range, but this will not cause any problem provided the engine performs satisfactorily and has a trouble-free transition.

One method of overcoming the mid-range tuning is to fit a fuel pump, as this will supply a constant, metered amount of fuel. A word of caution here. Fuel pumps and other added equipment serve a good purpose in certain circumstances but add to the paraphernalia that has to be maintained, set, adjusted and paid for which can tend to make a very serious business of a fun hobby. If you are going to spend thousands of hours building a perfect scale model, or compete in high stakes aerobatic competition and the like, then it is essential that you do everything possible to ensure maximum performance. This is definitely not warranted for the Sunday fun or sports flyer and certainly not for the beginner in the hobby, regardless of how deep your pockets are. Start off simply, enjoy and learn, then venture into the more complex side if you so desire.

Before any flight, when the carburettor has been adjusted, it is always sensible to hold the model nose high, at an angle of about 60°, and give full throttle. Hold it in this position for 15 seconds or so, to ensure that the engine shows no sign of leaning out. If it begins to lose revs, or sounds in any way distressed, you must richen the mixture, even if this gives rich running on the ground. Where there is a wide difference between the running on the ground (rich) and in the air (leaned out) the cause is more likely to be a plumbing problem, such as an air leak or the fuel tank situated too far away from the engine.

The final action before taking the model out for take-off should be to hold it nose high, with engines at full throttle, to ensure no leaning-off from the engines.

Chapter 5
Fault finding

QUITE SIMPLY, for an engine which has run satisfactorily before, if there is good fuel in the engine and a strong glow at the plug, it must fire. However, having the engine fire and getting it to run sweetly and smoothly is another matter. Problems will occur with the engine during its operating life and Brian Winch has devised a set of questions and answers to diagnose the problems.

Two-stroke problem diagnosis

Problem: Won't hold tune or overheats

Propeller—too large/small/out of balance/not tracking/loose

Tank—air leak/clunk too long and sucking against back of tank wall/rubbish in tank/vent or pressure nipple blocked/clunk off line/tank too high or low/tank too large/tubing split.

Fuel—contains water/too much—too little lubricant/dirt/foaming in tank/contaminated or stale/needs nitromethane.

Fuel lines—too small/thin wall collapsing/air leak/kinked or pressed/blockage/clogged filter/too large — sucking air.

Glow plug—incorrect heat range/faulty gasket/stem seal leaking/loose/faulty element/breaking down under load.

Engine—needs more running-in/crankshaft moved back—crankpin rubbing on backplate/air leak in crankcase due to loose bolts or crack/loose or warped head/debris in needle valve chamber/incorrect mixture setting/carb gasket leaking air/engine loose on mounts/varnish on liner/worn-damaged-misaligned crankshaft bearings/carb. too large/engine mount not square-distorting crankcase/muffler clogged or extended too far/insufficient air flow through cowl/ring sticking/prop driver rubbing on shaft housing/bent crankshaft/engine worn out.

Problem. Will run lean but not rich

Tank—too high or too low/sucking air/uneven pressure due to blocked vent or pressure line nipple.

Fuel—too much nitro for compression ratio/oil content too low/low grade methanol.

Fuel lines—too small/dirt in line/pinhole or kink/wall too thin.

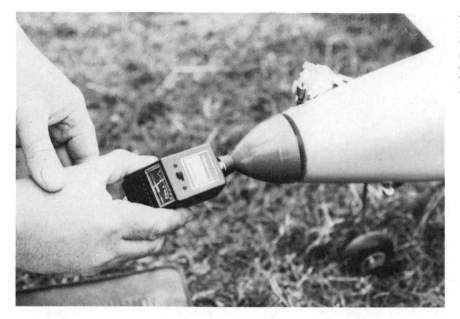

Tachometers, to check the speed of the engine, come in mechanical types or electronic optical versions. The latter are more versatile.

Glow plug—incorrect heat range—generally too cold/faulty/wrong length.

Engine—Loose or warped/crankcase bolts loose/air leak at carb. base/blockage in carb/high compression.
   If the engine will not run LEAN refer to first chart.

Problem. Will not continue running

Tank—Too high or too low/clunk line off tube or cracked/rubbish in tank/clunk too long — sucking against rear wall of tank/blocked vent/knot in clunk tube/clunk tube too stiff.

Fuel—incorrect mix/water in fuel/contaminated.

Fuel lines—blockage/clogged filter/too thin/restricted/air leak.

Glow plug—old or faulty/incorrect heat range.

Engine—blockage in carb./needle worn or 'O' rings defective/prop too large/

engine tight—needs more running-in/ engine worn out/blockage in muffler.

Problem. Will not start

Tank—empty

Fuel—water in fuel/contaminated/incorrect mixture

Fuel lines—total blockage/kinked or pressed/not connected to carb.

Glow plug—burnt out/plug lead circuit not complete/loose/flat battery/open circuit in plug leads or faulty connection/element broken.

Engine—needle valve closed or blocked/ loose or warped head/flooded/insufficient compression due to ring sticking in groove or engine worn out.

Four-stroke engines

All the above problems apply to four-stroke engines and they have some of their own.

Problem. Lack of power or hard to start

Incorrect valve rocker adjustment/valves not seating due to carbon on valve seat or build-up on exhaust valve stem/exhaust valve chamber full of carbon/incorrect timing/propeller too light/cam followers sticking/crankshaft bearings worn out or corroded badly/crankcase vent nipple blocked or extended with fuel tubing over two inches long/air leak in carb. induction tube or manifold.

Problem: Detonation or prop throwing.

Mixture too lean/choke closed or closing during operation/plug too hot/prop too light/too much oil in fuel/acetone in fuel (some methanols for full-size racing fuels contain a small percentage of castor oil and acetone)/oversize propeller/compression too high/propeller loose/flooded.

Problem. Engine won't idle.

Incorrect carb. setting/plug too cold/fuel too cold — replace 5 to 10% of the methanol with petrol or nitro-methane/engine not fully run in/compression too high/propeller too light/engine worn out/idle speed setting screw not set.

Problem. Excessive vibration—all engines

Propeller or spinner not balanced/propeller not tracking/crankshaft bearings worn or corroded/bent crankshaft/excessive wear in conrod/engine loose on mount/engine out of balance (home modifications?)/compression too high/idle too low/plug too hot/distorted crankcase due to crash damage or engine clamped in vice (oh moan!)/com-

mercial radial mount loose on firewall/firewall loose in airframe/home-made muffler too large or not supported.

Not directly related to running checks there are a couple of further items which may cause difficulties with the operation of four-stroke engines.

Timing in four-strokes

The timing mechanism in a four-stroke engine cannot slip. All components are mechanically locked in by keys or gears. The only way the timing can change is when you strip down the engine and you don't re-time it correctly.

Four-stroke breather nipples

The crankcase of the four-stroke engine (in fact, all engines) is, in effect, a timed pump. As the piston descends (comes down) it creates a positive pressure in the case. As it ascends (goes up) the pressure is negative. When the pressure is positive it forces the liquid in the

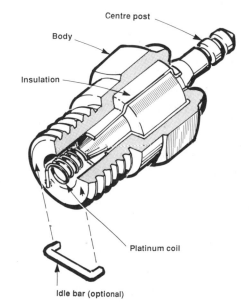

Construction of a glow plug.

crankcase out through the breather nipple.

On the negative pressure stroke it sucks in air. All this is changing 10,000 times per minute at 10,000 r.p.m. so it doesn't blow and suck for any great length of time. If you have a length of tubing on the breather nipple that is too long, the liquid blown out does not leave the tube before the negative pressure starts and it gets sucked in. As a general rule, the longest extension you should use is two inches. Check your engine to be certain that the waste oil is actually exiting the tube.

Glow plug problems and selection

The following notes will serve as a guide to sorting out plug problems but the best guide is to stick to the range recommended by the manufacturer of the engine.

The following symptoms indicate the plug is TOO HOT

When attempting to start the engine, it constantly backfires, throws the prop or runs in reverse.
The engine will not run smoothly on a rich setting or mid-range, particularly sport engines with a high nitro fuel.

The exhaust note is high-pitched and reedy. The engine will generally slow down or stop due to overheating.

At top r.p.m. the exhaust note is even but has a secondary sound like eggs frying or water sizzling in hot oil or fat. This is caused by lean running, plug too hot or too long. The fuel is pre-igniting and knocking the daylights out of the conrod!

The following symptoms indicate the plug is TOO COLD

The engine stops or loses more than about 300 r.p.m. when the starting battery is removed.

The engine is peaked out to top r.p.m. with the battery connected but stops when the battery leads are disconnected.

Engine goes off peak and runs rich and may even stop as if flooded.

Engine will not lean out into a smooth two-stroke sound—appears to be slightly rich.

Hard to start or gives very weak exhaust 'pop' only when flicked—little or no response when electric starter is used. Engine generally floods when starter is used.

If the engine can be coaxed to run it has a very uneven exhaust note.

Before making a final decision, take the plug out of the engine and check it with the battery. If the glow is weak, the battery may be on its last legs. No glow at all indicates the battery is dead flat.

There may be a few more problems which will occasionally raise their ugly heads, but the checks given above should give the answers to all but a handful of the causes.

Chapter 6
Care and maintenance

IT IS NATURAL for any modeller with an interest in things mechanical to want to know what makes an engine 'tick'. A natural extension of this curiosity is the desire to take an engine apart to examine all the components. Should a modeller, being a reasonably capable mechanic, take an engine apart? Will it be detrimental to the running of the engine and is there a risk of doing damage to the engine?

Never take an engine apart just for the sake of it, i.e. when the engine is operating perfectly well. Moving parts do become bedded in and they may not take up the exact same position when an engine is re-assembled. Do NOT become a tinkerer and a fiddler, making unnecessary adjustments to the engine and forever taking it to pieces. You will see these types on the flying field and they will surely have more problems than any of the other operators. On the other hand, there are times when it is necessary to disassemble the motor, to replace a damaged or worn part, or to check on the condition of components. As long as you tackle the job in a careful and logical sequence you shouldn't get into trouble or damage components. If you are at all doubtful it may be worth spending a tenner on an old engine and practising with that—you may even be able to get the old engine running!

Unscheduled arrivals

If you have the misfortune to crash a model and bury the engine in dirt or sand, dig it up carefully but DON'T TURN IT OVER. There will be grit forced into the engine but it will not do any damage provided the engine is not turned over to test for bent shafts, etc. (By turning over I mean do not revolve the crankshaft). Take the engine home as it is and either give it to the repairer complete with dirt (he will understand your good thinking) or, if you can, strip and assemble the engine yourself.

The first job is to wash off as much dirt as possible with soapy water and a toothbrush. Slosh the engine around in the water to remove as much as can be seen, then remove the carb and wash out any dirt in the carburettor section of the crankcase. Remove the backplate and wash out the inside of the engine. Completely strip the engine and wash each part in warm, soapy water. Rinse well, inspect for grit and damage, paying particular attention to the ballraces. Place all undamaged parts in a container and boil for about five minutes. Do not tip the parts out with the water as any grit will stay with the parts. Remove each part with tweezers and rinse well. Clean the container, making sure there is no grit left, and boil again. Tip the hot parts into a sieve, shake lightly and then tip onto a clean cloth. The heat will dry most parts but check for moisture, particularly in the races, and dry well. Oil all parts immediately to prevent rust. Replace the bearings and crankshaft in the front housing and check the shaft for truth. Replace any damaged parts and assemble the engine. A tip here: whenever you remove bolts from an engine for any reason, put a drop of oil in the threaded hole before replacing the bolt. This stops the bolt from binding—particularly in aluminium alloy—and reduces the wear on the threads.

When you have assembled the engine using plenty of oil, fit a prop and turn over slowly several times to check for binding or remaining foreign bodies. If all appears to be correct, check the engine on a test bench. If you notice more than usual vibration and you know the prop is balanced, it indicates that the shaft is bent. A slight bend in a shaft can be easily straightened but you need a fly press, a pair of centres and a dial test indicator so, unless you have this equipment lying around, send it to a qualified engine repairer.

Full servicing

You will need, depending on the engine, two or three well-shaped standard screwdrivers, one or two Phillips or

Breakdown of an Irvine two-stroke engine shows the relatively small number of parts. High quality castings are required for the crankcase. Carburettor body is from tough plastic.

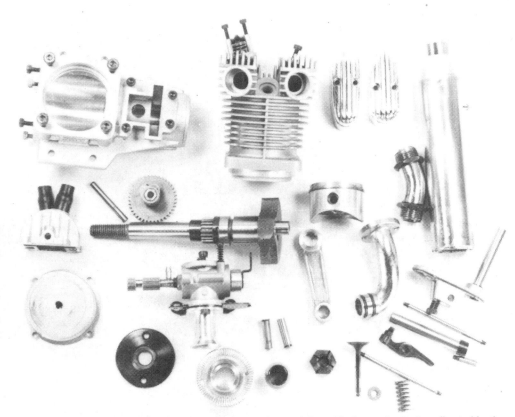

Component count is much higher in a four-stroke engine and the added complexity is reflected in the price. However, four-stroke engines are more economic to operate and, properly maintained, will last for many years.

Pozidrive screwdrivers (the business-end is a cross forming a point). Most engines now use Allen head bolts so you will need a range of Allen keys in the general range of 1.5mm to 3.5mm. A pair of fine point pliers for little bits and circlips, small spanners—*NO 'SHIFTING SPANNERS' ALLOWED, OR 'NUT RE-MOVING PLIERS'*—toothpicks or large darning needle and a larger than eyeball magnifying glass will be found quite useful. Ancillary equipment includes a block of clean hardwood about 3in. × 1in. × 6in. long, a shallow tray about 12in. square (the wife's scone tray is ideal), tissues, *CLEAN* cloth, fine grade lubricating oil and several clean salmon or cornbeef tins or margarine tubs, empty, of course, for storage of components. A pot and boiling water will be

needed, but these can be found and used in the kitchen when 'she who must be obeyed' is out shopping or gassing to the neighbour. You will need a frying pan and cookware cleaner for 'de-gunking' and a high grade gun oil will do a fair job for lubrication. *MAKE SURE* the cleaner is suitable for aluminium as a lot of kitchen cleaners contain caustic soda which will reduce your engine to a crankshaft, gudgeon pin, ring and some bolts floating in an evil smelling, grey, sludgy foam that *USED* to be the aluminium parts.

Now ... if you feel confident to tackle the taking apart of the engine and—more importantly—the reassembly of the parts, then go ahead. Remember that some engines, i.e. plain bearing, non-ringed types, are easier to manage

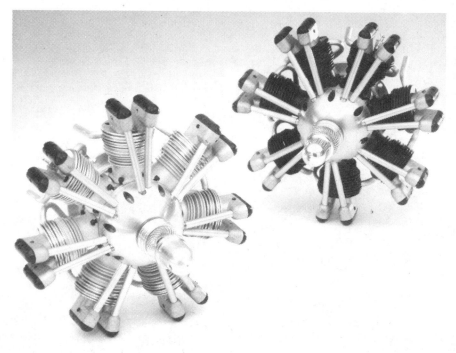

Five and seven cylinder four-stroke radial engines are now a practical proposition and although expensive are delightful to operate and hear.

than the more complex varieties. Should you feel distinctly apprehensive, swallow your pride and return the engine to the servicing agent, or obtain a book dealing specifically with the engine servicing.

Gaskets made easy

Use strong, brown paper such as nasty, official type envelopes for gasket material. Let us make a rear case gasket, for example. Clean and dry the rear end of the crankcase, press it onto a stamp pad, and then stamp the inked impression onto the brown paper. Small holes are best burnt through first with a hot wire. Cut the inner circle next with a sharp pointed modelling knife, then cut around the outside with sharp manicure (finger nail) scissors. Treat the finished job with light oil and fit into place. Simple, isn't it, after all the problems you have had in the past?

Four-stroke maintenance

Modellers seldom give a second thought to the problem of lubrication of a two-stroke engine. Provided the correct percentage of oil is included in the fuel, it is automatically assumed that all moving parts will be well lubricated. When they start to operate four-strokes, the fear of under-lubrication seem to take on levels out of proportion to the risks, probably due to unfounded rumours circulated by non-owners of four-stroke engines. Worries about adequate lubrication may be aggravated by the following considerations:

(a) Lower oil content in four-stroke fuel.
(b) Visible evidence of moving parts, i.e. valves and valve gear.
(c) Lack of crankcase induction (on most production engines) and the fear that bottom-end lubrication will be marginal.

Accepting the fact that the designers of four-stroke engines do know what they are about, and that the engines are well tested before they are put in production, you have little to fear of the engine seizing through lack of lubrication to vital parts.

Taking the latter point (c) first: no piston cylinder fit is 'perfect' to the extent that no fuel/air mixture or exhaust residue will pass from the upper cylinder to the crankcase. As a result of this leakage past the piston on the firing and exhaust strokes, the big-end gears and camshafts receive ample lubrication—the excess oil discharged through the crankcase breather nipple is sufficient proof of the oil present in the crankcase. This is equally true when the engine is mounted in the inverted position. Incidentally, as the crankcase of a four-stroke is normally unpressurised, it is not possible to use the breather nipple, or any other tapping, to pressurise the fuel tank. Few engines are fitted with silencers either, so the fuel in the tank will remain at atmospheric pressure.

Sufficient oil mist is released from the inlet and exhaust valves to keep the valve return spring, tappets and rocker bearings lubricated.

Tappet adjustment

R/C modellers can be roughly divided into two types, the mechanically minded and those principally interested in building and flying.

For the latter class, the thought of making engineering adjustments determined in thousandths of an inch may be a little perturbing. Fortunately, the adjustments to the tappets are not difficult or frequent (once the engine is run in) but mis-setting of the tappet clearance can seriously affect the per-

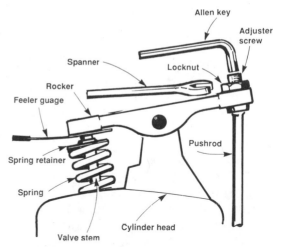

Tappet adjustment should be carried out when the engine is cold.

formance of the engine. With the small physical size of the valve gear of model four-strokes, it is inevitable that the valve lift is small, and the tappet clearance measured in micro-dimensions (typically 2–4 thou.).

Engines are supplied with the feeler gauges and most manufacturers also include spanners, screwdrivers or Allen keys to facilitate the tappet adjustments and give clear instructions on how to carry out the procedure.

Tappet clearance is set when the engine is cold and allowance is made for changes in clearance as the engine warms up. Do not set the clearances, using the feelers provided, when the engine is hot. Due to the very small clearances with the cold engine, it is important to make the adjustments precise, taking care when tightening the lock nuts not to disturb the carefully arrived at settings.

Readjustment of the tappets will be required a few times during the running-in period; a simple test for excessive clearance is to place fingers at each end of the rocket arm and press alternately on each end; any surplus movement will be easily detected. Once run-in, it should not be necessary to make frequent adjustments, although the clearances can be checked after every hour or so's running.

Cool running, modest r.p.m. and low vibration levels (provided the propeller is correctly balanced) are excellent conditions for an extended glow plug life and it is rare that plugs are 'blown' on four-strokes. That does not mean that the plug should be left in the engine *ad infinitum*—plugs do deteriorate and may be the cause of poor starting and running. Remove the plug occasionally and inspect the element. It should be bright and shiny—if it has a white crystalline appearance, change it.

Corrosion

The mere sound of the word sends shivers down the spine! How many of us take the trouble to clean the engine down after a flying session, and add a few drops of oil in the intake and plug hole?

With a two-stroke engine we will probably be lucky and suffer no major consequences, even when the engine remains unused for a lengthy period. To treat a four-stroke in this cavalier fashion does carry much greater risks, particularly with corrosion to the big-end, bearings, crankshaft and camshaft. Why should the corrosion risk be higher with four-strokes? With any engine a small proportion of the combustion gases get past the piston (as described in lubrication) and these gases contain harmful substances that, when condensed into acids, are highly corrosive. In a two-stroke engine, the gases are scavenged from the crankcase when the piston descends, compressing the gases in the crankcase (including the fresh fuel/air charge) and forcing them up the transfer port to the cylinder.

There is no similar scavenging effect in a four-stroke and, as the engine cools, the dew point is reached and the contaminants condense into an acid. It does not take much imagination to visualise the results of leaving the engine in this stage for any length of time.

To eliminate the risks of corrosion, the engine should be run at full bore, at the end of the day's flying, and then stopped by removing the fuel line to the carburettor (or pinching it closed with a pair of surgical tweezers). Give the engine a chance to warm up thoroughly before this action is taken. When the engine is cool enough to handle, remove the glow plug and inject a few drops of oil into the plug hole and through the crankcase breathing nipple. Turn the engine over a dozen times to ensure that the oil is well dispersed. When the engine is to be set aside for a longer period, i.e. a month or more, it is advisable to remove the backplate, or, as in the case of Enya engines, the front housing, wash the engine out and oil thoroughly. Do not use an alcohol for cleaning the interior of the engine as this will only attract more moisture. There are suitable purpose-designed products, such as Model Technic's 'Water Displacing Oil', that can be used in the engine to serve the same purpose followed by a final application of mineral oil (e.g. 3-in-1 or a 'Lay-up' oil). Rotate the crankshaft to distribute the oil throughout the engine, replace the covers and plug and cover the engine to protect it from dust. These elementary precautions will protect the engine from the dreaded rust—it may even become a habit for all of our engines! For those modellers wishing to go further into the maintenance and repair of four-stroke engines we recommend purchasing one of the specialist books on four-stroke engines.

Chapter 7
Propeller selection

IF YOU THINK that there is a wide selection of model engines to choose from, wait until you get to propellers! With such a wide variety of commercial propellers to make our choice from, how do we go about picking the one that will be ideal for our engine? In a nutshell, select the prop that gives your *model* the best performance.

The prop is the load for your engine. Without it the engine would self-destruct very quickly so, before we delve into prop sizes, let us check the attachment of them to the engine. The commonest method used for attaching the propeller to an engine is a simple nut and washer. The washer is quite important as it prevents the nut biting into the prop and gives a larger surface area for its holding properties. Try to keep the original washer as it is the right size for the shaft and the tapered face prevents it dishing when the nut is tightened. If you do lose it, it is best to purchase the correct replacement for the reasons stated above. If this is not possible for some reason, *PLEASE* do not use a ⅜in. washer on a ¼in. shaft. It is bound to run off centre and the imbalance of weight is fatal to bearing surfaces in the engine.

The prop should be a very neat fit on the shaft—I like mine to just screw on or, at least, to be a firm, push fit. If the hole in the prop is ¹⁄₁₆ in. oversize you can bet the prop will be ¹⁄₃₂ in. too far one way and this is way out of balance.

For a ¼in. steel nut, the engineering recommendation is seven inches of leverage. As we are tightening onto wood or plastic, we can get sufficient tightness with a little less than this. Don't use pliers, multi-grips or adjustable (shifting) spanners as these will burr the corners of the nut. The best possible engine nut spanner is like a small dumbbell weight with the ball ends perforated with hexagon holes and is generally available from cycle shops.

If you use a wood prop, tighten up quite snugly initially then, after a couple of runs, retighten. The wood in the hub compresses a little with time and your prop becomes loose. Check this from time to time, (if you are fortunate enough to keep a wood prop for any length of time!) as the fuel soaking into the wood makes it a bit spongy and, again the prop could spin loose. If you lose a prop or loosen a prop in flight, more often than not the engine will continue to run. This is called a 'shaft run'—the engine is running without a load and unless the R/C throttle is closed damage will be caused to the engine. Occasionally, an engine will backfire or cough in flight and the nut, washer and prop will take off for parts unknown. If you pull the throttle off quickly enough you can prevent a shaft run but the chances of finding the missing parts are very slim. If you have an engine that is inclined to 'spit and cough' occasionally, fit a Nylock nut for the shaft nut.

With safety in mind, it is now recommended that you fit a spinner or spinner nut to your engine. The reason behind this is that, if your model should hit a person, the round end of the spinner or spinner nut will, hopefully, only cause bruising where a bare shaft would definitely cause an open wound. The spinner nut is in the shape of a bowler hat—narrow brim, round crown—and is tightened by inserting a metal rod through a hole drilled through the 'crown'.

Materials used in propeller manufacture

Modellers have been offered props in a variety of materials over the years including wood, aluminium, hard rubber, various plastics, nylon and a material called Hydulignum. Of these only the wood and nylon remain today. With the advance in power of model engines, all the other materials were considered too dangerous for use. These days we are offered glass reinforced plastics (GRP or fibreglass), reinforced

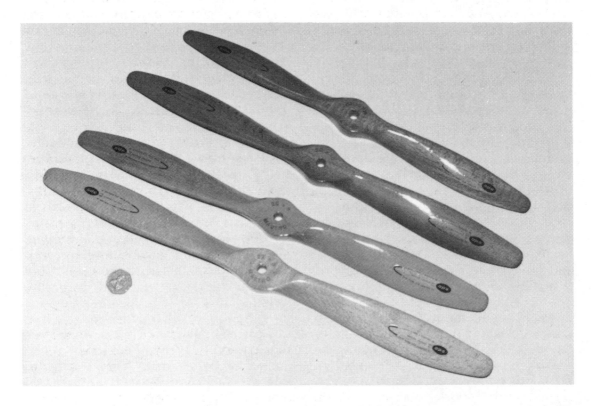

Wooden propellers remain the most popular with 'serious' modellers, but, whatever the type of propeller used, it should be sound and free from defects.

nylon, carbon fibre reinforced plastic and, of course, wood for prop material. There are many factors to consider when choosing the material from which your prop is manufactured. Some of the reinforced props are so sturdy that they could bend a crankshaft in a crash and all of them will inflict severe injuries to flesh without breaking. On the other hand, they are usually low in price and long-lasting due to the fact they will survive ground contact on rough landings without (generally) breaking. Most of them come complete with razor sharp edges from the mould joint and need smoothing with fine sandpaper before use. They should always be checked for balance. Wood props are considered more efficient and are easily reworked or customised and are more likely to break before inflicting severe injuries to stray fingers or hands. They are also easily damaged by bumping or rough landings. In use, they are most unlikely to shed a blade if they are in good condition. Balance the factors and make your choice.

Size

The size to suit your engine is advised in the manufacturer's instruction sheet and this is a good starting point. Propeller performance is influenced by the type of model, the speed required, the cowl or frontal area of the model, the performance or aerobatic manoeuvres to be flown, acceleration and type of engine. Contrary to popular belief, the cowl or frontal area of a model does not reduce the efficiency of a prop. It is not the air behind the prop that does the work, it is the air in front that the prop 'bites' into that gives forward motion. The frontal area can, however, in some instances, create considerable wind resistance to reduce forward speed. On

the other hand, it has been proved that the round cowl of the type fitted around radial engines actually *increases* speed due to the drag effect acting in a similar manner to an airfoil.

Consider two different models. First off, a fully rigged, semi-scale biplane. Lots of parasitic drag from the cabanes and rigging wires, two wings to get working and a fair speed required for take-off and landing. The propeller needed for this type of model is one with a large diameter and a fine pitch. With this combination your forward speed is low but acceleration and pulling power are increased with a high revving engine. Now consider a pylon model. Acceleration from the prop is not required as this is taken care of by the sleek lines of the model and the high speed of the engine. Once in the air the throttle is wide open and the model needs maximum speed. As the model rounds the pylons, it is not acceleration that makes it appear to be on rails but high speed inertia and maximum streamlining of the model. The models fly on coarse pitch props. Aerobatics fliers require an engine and prop combination that will give a nice even speed throughout the flight. Watch a good pattern flyer performing and you will see a constant speed almost throughout the entire flight. These models trade off acceleration and high speed for pure power and constant speed in all attitudes. A result of this combination is that the engines are quieter due to the lower rpm and the prop noise is down due to lower tip speed.

Where does all this leave us? The point is that no standard can be set for all engines and all types of models. Start off with the standard prop for the engine size and see how the model performs. If you need more acceleration, increase the diameter and reduce the pitch in small increments. If your model is too slow in flight, increase the pitch on the standard prop size but be wary of decreasing the diameter too severely as this may cause the prop to be inefficient.

Balance

EVERY prop needs to be balanced before initial use, after any modifications, e.g. tip painting or lacquering. A prop that is a few grams out of balance can destroy an engine or wrench it out of the mounting. I have seen modellers attempt to balance props on the edge of a pocket-knife (in the wind), on the shaft of a screwdriver and on a length of twine threaded through the shaft hole. None of these methods is suitable and should not be used. Proprietary and home-made balancers include (a) a rod on the edge of two razor blades, (b) a rod set at the point where two metal discs meet and (c) two tapered nuts on a shaft held in the fingers. Unless the first two mentioned are manufactured with the precision of a jewelled movement watch they are of little use and the third method fails because of the fingers. Unless the shaft is at absolute 90° (for 360° rotation) to the bearings (fingers), the bias in any direction will influence the lie of the blades and this will show up as imbalance which will not be corrected. The only true method of total balance checking is to use a needle point in a conical receiver, such as the Du Bro prop balancer. This unit consists of an aluminium tube with knurled caps threaded into each end. One cap has a fine pointed needle and the other has a conical depression. The cap with the conical depression is screwed into the shaft hole of the prop squarely and the needle end is set on a true surface. A true surface may be the flat bed of a lathe, milling machine, drill press, marking off table and similar. Every modeller may not have access to the true surfaces mentioned, but possibly own or can borrow a spirit level. Using a piece of flat metal, plate glass or a very smooth piece of painted timber about 3in. square, you can set this up with the level to get a true surface.

When you have the needle set up, place the prop over the point so that it (the point) is located in the conical depression. Any portion of the prop that dips down is heavier than its opposite side and must be lightened to create a balance. The beauty of the needle method is that it balances all points of the prop—lengthways along the blades and crossways across the hub—and it is the second point where all other balancers fall short. The failure of the Du Bro unit is that the screw-in hub will only fit

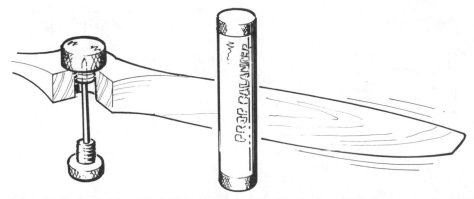

Propeller balancing is absolutely essential for smooth running. The Du Bro type balancer gives true balancing in all directions.

Three-bladed propellers are almost as efficient as equivalent two-bladed types and are useful where ground clearance is minimal and for some scale subjects.

a ¼in. shaft hole and many props are made with smaller or larger than ¼in. holes. In these instances you need adapters and, as these are beyond the scope of modellers who don't have a lathe, we have to use the next best method.

A starting point

After reading to this stage you will understand that the prop sizes listed are a guide only. Your engine will work with them and they will not cause overloading but they may not necessarily be the best prop for your application or model.

Diesel engines

.8 and 1cc	7 × 4
149 (1½)cc	7 × 6
249 (2½)cc	9 × 4
3cc (.19ci)	10 × 4
5cc (.29–30ci)	11 × 4

Glow plug engines

1.6cc (.10ci)	7 × 6
2.5cc (.15ci)	8 × 4
3.3cc (.20ci)	9 × 4
4.1cc (.25ci)	9 × 6
5cc (.30ci)	10 × 5
6.6cc (.40ci)	10 × 6
7.5cc (.45ci)	11 × 6
10cc (.60ci)	11 × 7
13.3cc (.80ci)	12 × 6

Spark ignition

15 to 20% to the next largest diameter of the recommended size for glow plug engines.

Four-stroke

Wide scope for experiment.
Refer to instructions or next size up from GLOW chart.

Bear in mind that the prop is the flywheel or load of your engine. If the load is too light, the engine will be difficult to start and will rev beyond the recommended limit, causing strain and damage. If you overload the engine with a prop too large it will run hot and also cause mechanical damage—generally a broken crankshaft or conrod. While a glowplug engine will generally tolerate light loads, within reason, both the diesel and the four-stroke require a reasonable load to function correctly. A light load on a diesel engine causes difficult starting and it becomes very 'bitey' on the fingers. Four-stroke en-gines kick back and throw props loose if the load is too light. They can kick so hard that they can shed a blade on starting and this can be quite startling and dangerous. Aim for a prop diameter that will allow the engine to run up to 90% of the recommended operating r.p.m. as set out in the instructions. Once your model is in the air, the static load reduces and you will gain the 10% as the engine unloads. By doing this you can be reasonably assured that the engine will not over-rev in the air and shorten its life.

Horizontally opposed twin engines will give smoother running than a similar sized single cylinder engine. They also have more compact dimensions and—to most modeller's ears—a more pleasant exhaust note.

Chapter 8
Fuels

THE FUEL, whether it is for glow, diesel or spark ignition model engines, serves two purposes. It provides the 'energy' to operate the engine and it provides lubrication for the moving parts. All of the present generation of commercial model aero engines use a fuel which includes a lubricating oil; we have not, as yet, reached the stage where the oil is separated (as would be the case with the family car except in some hand-built spark ignition engines). It is with the oils, particularly synthetics, and additives that most development has taken place in the past few years, resulting in a degree of controversy and rumours regarding the suitability of some fuels.

Oil performs two important functions: it provides a barrier against metal-to-metal friction to reduce wear and it carries away considerable engine heat. These factors must be considered when experimenting with different oils. In all engines we have certain points that are subject to the hammer effect. When the piston changes direction, the tolerances in the big and little end of the rod open and close as does the gudgeon pin in the piston. In a four-stroke we also have the cam-followers on the cams and, to a lesser extent, the teeth on the gear train. At 10,000 rpm the parts hammer 20,000 times per minute.

No matter what is tried, castor oil still reigns supreme. Nothing can beat it for lubricating properties and lean run protection. It does, however, fall short in two areas—dreadful gunk that sprays all over the model and its nasty habit of going solid if left to dry out in an engine.

Over the last three or four years a number of synthetic oils that are soluble in alcohol fuels have been tried. Some of these oils are great for modellers' use as they are used at low percentages, don't 'gunk-up' the model and give perfect after-run protection to the engine. One problem some of them suffer from is that they burn at a lower temperature than castor and may not give the needed protection on lean runs. Some of them even aid in combustion and help the engine unload considerably once the model is in motion.

However, there is still a vast amount of experiment and development work to be carried out before we find a synthetic oil with all the good properties of castor oil. Until then, fuels (especially if they are cheaper than the norm) with synthetic oils should be treated with caution. There *are* synthetic oils which have been proven in testing, such as Synlube and, for spark ignition, Silkolene, and no doubt there are many others. Just make sure that the oil content of the fuel is adequate and the quality is good. This advice also applies to castor-based fuels where a second-grade oil can break down more quickly and certainly cause more 'varnishing' of the piston and liner.

If you are an experienced modeller and have an empathy with engines you are unlikely to damage an engine through misuse. You may safely operate on lower oil contents.

Your engines will run on a lot less oil—and could do so if it were not for one little gadget on all engines—the needle valve. Because the tuning of the air/fuel ratio is left to often inexperienced operators, the manufacturers have brain-washed us into accepting that we must use so much oil. The oil is the only protection the engine has when you tune it too lean. The engine temperature rises alarmingly on a lean run and the high flash-point of the castor provides some measure of protection.

So, you can experiment with different oils and lower oil contents in the fuel; modern engines are more tolerant of lower oil contents than some of the older designs and it is accepted now that four-stroke engines run much better on lower oil content. Most modellers will want to keep at least a 2% castor content in the fuel, regardless of the synthetic oil used, just as an insurance against a lean run. If you are not sure what you should use and fiddle with the needle valve, use 20% castor for two-strokes and 15% for four-strokes.

One point to remember is that you experiment with fuel mixes at your own risk, as you are the person tuning the mixture and this makes a big difference.

The power source

There does not seem to have been a successful alternative, for glow engines, to methanol as the actual fuel content. Many substitutes have been tried, either as a total replacement, or as a percentage fuel, often with disastrous results.

Additives for glow fuels

Like oils, many additives have been tried over the years in the search for the elusive extra revs. Again, these experiments often had sad results. Most of the additives are in the aromatic nitrous

Be confident and bold—but careful—with your starting. Large engines need a substantial and rapid swing. Being tentative is more likely to cause a 'back-fire'—but this modeller obviously knows his engine as he wears no protective gear!

category. Nitro-benzene wrecks your kidneys, nitro-propane evaporates before you can use it, nitro-methane reverts to nitric acid compounds to chew engines up and amyl-nitrate causes blinding headaches and cardiac acceleration. All are dangerous to your health (as is methanol) and, if used, extreme caution must be exercised. Most of the chemicals react in similar fashion— they release more oxygen under combustion. As the oxygen is increased the engine requires more fuel to maintain the air fuel ratio. As this increases, theoretically, up goes the rpm. Another thing they have in common is the high cost.

Nitro-methane is frequently recommended for four-stroke engines, often as a 10% content. This may or may not be necessary, or may only be desirable for easier starting in cold weather. If you are not certain whether a nitro content is essential (as it is with some of the small capacity high rpm engines) just try the engine on straight fuel and see what happens. The alternative is certainly a lot cheaper and eliminates most of the worries about internal corrosion.

Diesel engine fuels

Diesel engines need heat and pressure to ignite the fuel, and lubrication for the obvious reasons. Castor provides adequate lubrication and its high viscosity (measure of pourability, or how thick it is) provides the necessary piston/liner seal. Kerosene (paraffin) has the correct flash point for this type of combustion so it is right for the fuel content. All we

need is heat and the engine provides this once it gets going. The fact that the engine is obviously cold when first started is the main reason we use ether as this acts as an igniter under compression. Some diesels, when warmed up, will run without the ether in the fuel and, indeed, on straight kerosene, but the changeover is fiddly and the combustion temperature is quite critical.

A problem that crops up with the use of castor as a lubricant in lapped piston engines, slow revving engines and engines run rich at slow rpm (as is the case quite often with diesels) is that of varnishing. The castor forms a glazed surface on the liner and piston which reduces the working clearance and builds up heat. For this reason alone it is worthwhile trying some of the modern synthetic oils now available. A diesel engine will run quite well on a surprisingly low oil content if it has a good piston seal. If it wasn't for the plain bearings on the conrod, you could run a ball-race shaft diesel on kerosene and ether alone. The ether content can also

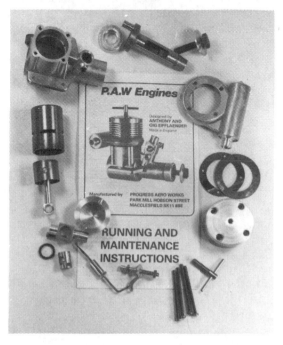

Dismantled PAW diesel engine illustrates the essential simplicity of this design, note the annular exhaust collecting ring for the small silencer chamber. Diesels are fairly quiet in operation.

Glow engines can be converted to spark ignition, as illustrated with this Mini-Mag unit fitted to an Enya four-stroke engine. Economy of these conversions is quite remarkable.

be reduced as it is only needed for ignition. Acetone improver (cetane in diesel fuels = octane in petrol fuels) such as amyl nitrite (or nitrate) or isopropyl nitrate used at about 2–3%, will allow you to reduce the content even further.

Probably the best known diesel additive is nitro-benzene (oil of myrrbane) but it is considered to be too dangerous to use these days.

To run a new diesel engine try the 1 : 1 : 1 mix; later, you might like to try 1 oil–3 kerosene–1 ether. Make your experimental batches in small amounts of about 10 ml (measure with a syringe) at a time. This way you will have enough to indicate if it works and if it doesn't, you can add it to the next large batch of fuel you make to save wasting it. Another way to go is to mix 3 parts kerosene to 1 part ether and add the recommended percentage of synthetic oil as set out in the instructions for use (of the oil). The diesel engine is easy on fuel experimenters as it gives plenty of warning if it is not happy. If it starts to get hot it runs hard and has a distinct knock. The moment you notice this, release the compression and disconnect the fuel line. The indication will be that the engine is overcompressed when it reaches operating temperature or that it needs more lubrication. For this reason do all experiments on the bench and stand close by ready for action. Of course, the engine will overheat and knock if the prop load is too great, so stick to the recommended sizes. If the engine will run for six or seven minutes smoothly without a change in exhaust note or becoming unduly hot, you could be on the right track with the fuel mix.

Spark ignition

Petrol engines, as spark ignition motors are frequently described, operate on a standard petrol/oil mix, much as your motor mower does. Although unleaded petrol is being introduced throughout the world, this is not the fuel for us; it will ruin the valve seatings. Use premium or super grade of petrol and a racing grade oil (although 'sparkies' will also run on glow fuel).

The first problem is that the engine runs considerably hotter than a glow engine so we need an oil that has a high flash point so that it will not burn during combustion and leave the engine without lubrication. So what oil is suitable? The most quoted fuel mix from way back is 3 or 4 to one of 70 weight (SAE) engine oil. The 3 or 4 is, of course, petrol. Now, engine oil is the oil we put in the sump of our car and, as such, it is not designed for burning or dilution. But some of the two-stroke and synthetic two-stroke oils won't have had enough body to provide the protection needed in a model. Remember that we are diluting the oil considerably to the point where

we are running about SAE 5 oil through the engine, which is far too light for a plain bearing conrod and cam-followers. Castor oil, the old standby, again comes to the fore and solves all our problems, only now we have gooey models!

You can use some of the synthetics that have polymers suitable for heavy duty use. Take positive steps to ascertain if a brand of oil is suitable for the type of work it will get in a spark ignition engine. The mixture of synthetics and castor oil (as with glow fuel) mixed with petrol is a good fuel. Synthetics of the right type, such as Synlube or Silkolene Pro 2 racing oil, can be used at ratios of 20:1 for running-in and 30:1 for normal operation.

If the foregoing seems a little complicated, here are three mixes you can try with your spark ignition engine, bearing

A real fire-breather. Twin pulse jet R/C model is an awesome sight—and sound—in the air but should be left to the experts to operate. High speeds, volatile fuels and high temperatures need cautious handling.

in mind that other synthetic oils will also be suitable for fuel mixes.

a. Castor/Petrol at 15 to 18%.
b. 2 parts Synlube, 1 part Castor used at 5% with petrol.
c. Silkolene Pro 2 at 30:1 ratio.

Any one of the mixtures will provide all that is necessary for your engine so it's up to you now to make *your* choice.

Two points to finish the petrol problem. One: petrol destroys rubber and silicone so you will have to use plastic or neoprene tubing and *don't forget the clunk tube in the tank*. Two: Do a comprehensive ground/radio check with the engine running in case of ignition interference. Just one other thing: *petrol is very dangerous—take extra care*.

Appendix 1

**Typical examples
of late 1980s
engine design**

OS 40FB Max

Tartan Single Glow 22cc

Webra 74-80

Super Tigre 2000

Saito FHA65 four-stroke

Tartan Twin 44cc

Enya 40cc

Index

Balancing propellers	52	Glow fuels	56
Bench testing	25	Glow plugs	42
Carburettors	18	Installing engines	31
Cleaning	43	Installing fuel tanks	35
Corrosion prevention	48		
		Multi-cylinder engine layouts	18
Diesel engine starting	30		
Diesel fuels	57	Propeller selection	49
Dismantling engines	23	Propeller types and sizes	50
Engine mounts	33	Servicing	44
Engine starting	26	Silencers	21
		Spark ignition	11
Fault finding	39	Spark ignition fuels	58
Four-stroke engine operation	15 & 28	Starter batteries	27
Fuel filters	35	Starters	26
Fuel tanks	34		
		Tappet adjustment	47
Gaskets	46	Tuned pipe silencers	22
Glossary of terms	11	Two-stroke engine operation	17 & 26

Subscribe now...

here's 4 good reasons why!

Within each issue these four informative magazines provide the expertise, advice and inspiration you need to keep abreast of developments in the exciting field of model aviation.

With regular new designs to build, practical features that take the mysteries out of construction, reports and detailed descriptions of the techniques and ideas of the pioneering aircraft modellers all over the world – they represent four of the very best reasons for taking out a subscription.

You need never miss a single issue or a single minute of aeromodelling pleasure again!

	U.K.	Europe	Middle East	Far East	Rest of World
Aeromodeller *Published monthly*	£23.40	£28.20	£28.40	£30.20	£28.70
Radio Modeller *Published monthly*	£15.60	£21.20	£21.40	£23.60	£21.80
RCM&E *Published monthly*	£15.60	£21.60	£21.80	£24.00	£22.20
Radio Control Scale Aircraft *Published quarterly*	£9.00	£11.10	£11.20	£12.00	£11.30

Your remittance with delivery details should be sent to:

The Subscriptions Manager (CG/14)
Argus Specialist Publications
1 Golden Square LONDON W1R 3AB.